# THE
# TRAVELS OF
# REVEREND
# ÓLAFUR
# EGILSSON

THE CATHOLIC
UNIVERSITY
OF AMERICA
PRESS

Washington, D.C.

# THE TRAVELS OF REVEREND ÓLAFUR EGILSSON

The Story of the
Barbary Corsair Raid on
Iceland in 1627

TRANSLATED FROM
THE ORIGINAL ICELANDIC TEXT
AND EDITED BY

Karl Smári Hreinsson &
Adam Nichols

English translation Copyright © 2008
Karl Smári Hreinsson and Adam Nichols
Original English edition © 2008
Fjölvi ehf, Reykjavík, Iceland
Second English edition © [2011]
Saga Akademía ehf, Keflavík, Iceland

The paper used in this publication meets the minimum
requirements of American National Standards for Information
Science—Permanence of Paper for Printed Library Materials,
ANSI Z39.48-1984.

∞

Cataloging-in-Publication Data available from the
Library of Congress
ISBN 978-0-8132-2869-3

THIS BOOK IS FOR ÞÓRDUR TÓMASSON
(Dr. h.c.), founder and curator of the Skógar District Museum
in South Iceland, for his lifelong interest in the
history of the *Tyrkjaránið*. At the age of 94, he is still
indefatigably researching and writing.

*Karl Smári Hreinsson*

THIS BOOK IS FOR MY WIFE,
who never—ever—complains about the piles of books,
magazines, and journals I constantly leave lying about and who
accepts with equanimity the endless hours I spend fooling
around with (digital) pen and paper. Bless her.

*Adam Nichols*

# Contents

☙

## THE TRAVELS OF REVEREND ÓLAFUR EGILSSON

# CONTENTS

# CONTENTS

# CONTENTS

## LETTERS, APPENDIXES, SUGGESTIONS FOR FURTHER READING & INDEX

# Illustrations

## MAPS

## IMAGES

# ILLUSTRATIONS

# Acknowledgments ❧

WE WOULD LIKE TO THANK the following people for their help in the preparation of the *The Travels of Reverend Ólafur Egilsson* and accompanying letters. Dr. Bernard Lewis, professor emeritus, Princeton University, read the manuscript and gave us invaluable advice. Dr. Halldór Baldursson's astute suggestions, based on his expertise in Early Modern naval history, enabled us to improve our translation. Dr. Þorsteinn Helgason, associate professor of history at the University of Iceland, and a leading Icelandic expert on the *Tyrkjaránið*, advised us in many ways. Steinunn Jóhannesdóttir, freelance writer and novelist, shared her extensive knowledge of the *Tyrkjaránið* with us. The late Hjálmar Sveinsson, a farmer and self-taught scholar from North Iceland (one of many Icelandic farmers who gained outstanding knowledge of Icelandic history and literature through lifelong independent study), helped us with many difficult old Icelandic words. Jón Kristvin Margeirsson, in Reykjavík, provided information about currency values and other aspects of the seventeenth century. Iiris and Kjell Geelnard helped clarify the biblical references in the *The Travels*. Finally, Suzanna Stephens advised us on the Spanish language, and Jade Carameaux-Jurewicz advised us on French and Spanish. We would also like to express our appreciation to Trevor Lipscombe, director of the Catholic University of America Press, as well as to Brian Roach, Tanjam Jacobson, and Theresa Walker, also of the CUA Press, and to Kate Stern, copy editor extraordinaire.

# Introduction ⳍ

THE TRAVELS OF REVEREND ÓLAFUR EGILSSON (known
in Iceland as *Reisubók Séra Ólafs Egilssonar*) is a well-known
classic of seventeenth century Icelandic literature, but it has
never before been translated into English.[1] It tells an altogether
remarkable story.

In the summer of 1627, Barbary corsairs from Algiers and
Salé (on the Atlantic coast of what is now Morocco) descended
upon Iceland.[2] This dramatic event is known in Iceland as the
*Tyrkjaránið*—the Turkish Raid.[3] Accounts differ, but it is generally believed that one ship came from Salé and attacked the

1. "Ólafur" is pronounced "*Oh*-laver." "Egilsson" is pronounced "*Ay*-yill-son."
2. "Barbary" was the general term used by seventeenth century Europeans to
refer to the North African Mediterranean coast west of Egypt, the area that includes the modern countries of Libya, Tunisia, Algeria, and Morocco. The word
is not used very much today except in the phrase "Barbary corsairs" or "Barbary
pirates." We use "Maghreb" to refer to this region. Maghreb comes from an Arabic
term meaning "place of the setting sun" and so "place of the west," since that part
of the world was located westwards of the Arabic speakers who named it.
3. Tyrkjaránið is pronounced "*Tirk*-ya-rawn-ith," with the *th* pronounced as
in "the." The ð is the letter eth (lower case, ð; upper case, Ð), not found in the
modern English alphabet. It represents the voiced "th" sound in words like "the"
or "these." The name Tyrkjaránið comes from the fact that seventeenth century
Icelanders (and Europeans in general) referred to all Muslims, whether from the
actual territory of the Ottoman Empire itself (centered in what is now modern
Turkey) or the outlying areas of North Africa, as "Turks."

xv

southwest corner of the island, while three ships came from Algiers and attacked the southeast coast and the Westman Islands, off the south coast. As many as forty or more people were killed in the raid and close to four hundred in total were taken away to North Africa to be sold into slavery. Reverend Ólafur and his family were among those captured on the Westman Islands.

The islanders ended up in Algiers. Reverend Ólafur did not stay there very long, though, for his captors chose to send him off to arrange ransoms for his family and the other Icelanders. They provided him with a letter of safe-conduct (to prevent other corsairs from interfering with his task in case a ship he was on should be attacked) and sent him on his way. He then traveled alone—without money or support—across the Mediterranean, through Italy and France, to Holland, and, finally, to Denmark (Iceland was a Danish possession in those days) to petition the Danish king for ransom funds. Denmark was faring badly in the Thirty Years' War at the time, however, and the royal coffers were empty. Reverend Ólafur had to return to Iceland alone, making landfall on the Westman Islands on July 6, 1628, slightly under a year after his original capture.

It may come as a surprise to some that Barbary corsairs, operating out of ports along the Maghreb, should have been raiding Iceland, of all places. Who exactly were these corsairs, and what prompted them to launch a raid on a place so very far away?[4] Perhaps the best way to answer that question is to begin by saying what they were not.

They were not "pirates," at least not the sort of buccaneering

4. The distance is over 2,000 miles (3,200 kilometers).

freebooters—like Captain Kidd or Blackbeard—that the word *pirate* typically brings to mind. Barbary corsairs certainly behaved like pirates, in that they boarded ships and took by force everything they could (often including the ships themselves), but they were not lone wolfs out purely for illicit personal profit. And though there was an element of jihad in the corsair enterprise, the situation was not a simple antithetical "clash of civilizations"—Maghrebi Muslims versus European Christians—acted out on the high seas. Things were more complicated than that on both counts.

It is important to remember that the seventeenth century world was very different from our own. We casually refer to sixteenth/seventeenth century European "countries" using familiar names—Iceland, England, Denmark, France, Germany, Holland, Italy, Portugal, Spain—and the very familiarity of these names makes it all too easy to forget that these were not what we would today recognize as nation-states. Among other things, they typically did not have standing armies and navies of the size and permanence we now take for granted. As a result, during the sustained conflicts that marked much of the sixteenth century, governments resorted to merchant corporations, mercenary armies, and privateers to achieve their goals.[5]

Privateers were private individuals/ships that had received a commission of war—customarily referred to as a "letter of marque and reprisal"—from a government or monarch to attack and seize foreign vessels. The proceeds would then typically be split between the private backer(s) of the privateering expedition and the government or monarch. Among other

5. It is interesting to note that modern governments seem to be reviving the use of private actors to achieve military goals (though for a very different set of reasons). Such actors used to be called privateers or mercenaries; now they are referred to as contractors.

things, this stratagem enabled the ruling powers to muster an increased number of armed ships against an enemy without having to incur the extra expense of permanently enlarging their existing navies. During the varied conflicts in the sixteenth century, privateering was a standard practice. Scores of English sea dogs, French *filibustiers*, and Dutch *watergeuzen* hunted both sides of the Atlantic, enriching both themselves and their governments—a system that continued, in varying forms, into the nineteenth century.

The Barbary corsairs were also, in their way, a species of privateer. After the conquest of Constantinople in 1453, the Ottoman Empire expanded on both shores of the Mediterranean basin—into the Balkans and across North Africa. In Reverend Ólafur's day, cities like Algiers were under the rule of the Ottoman Porte.[6] As various European powers negotiated treaties with the Porte, the Maghrebi corsairs, as Ottoman subjects, were supposed to abide by these treaties and attack only those ships belonging to powers with which the Porte had not entered into treaties. As well, some European powers arranged individual treaties with corsair cities, paying an annual tribute to keep their ships safe, so Barbary corsairs did not simply attack all and sundry. They were as constrained as any privateer—at least in theory. How scrupulously they abided by these constraints is, of course, another question.

Barbary corsairs had financial backers who expected to make a profit. Each expedition was carefully financed, and the spoils meticulously accounted for and shared out. In this aspect of things, Barbary corsairs were indistinguishable from European privateers. But corsairs were also Muslim—at least a substan-

---

6. The term "Ottoman Porte" (also Sublime Porte) is an example of metonymy (like using "the Crown" to refer to a monarch). It refers to the gate that gave access to the main government buildings in Istanbul.

tial portion of them were—and their beliefs undeniably played a role in these undertakings. The Spanish *Reconquista*, culminating in the expulsion of resident Muslims from Granada in 1492, ushered in a period of Spanish expansion along the Maghreb, and by the beginning of the second decade of the sixteenth century, towns from Oran to Algiers to Tripoli were either captured and occupied or had signed treaties of capitulation. In the larger world, this was all part of the struggle between the Spanish/ Habsburg and Ottoman empires for hegemony in the Mediterranean basin. For the Maghrebi, however, it was more personal. Hordes of displaced, vengeful Spanish Muslims flooded Maghrebi towns, and the *dar al-Islam* was felt to be under attack by Christian—Spanish—invaders.[7]

In obedience to the Muslim tradition requiring believers to aid their brothers in whatever part of the dar al-Islam may be threatened, volunteers from other parts of the Islamic world rushed to help repel the infidel invaders—the very essence of jihad (in this case, also, *al-jihad fil-bahr*, the holy war at sea). This is the time of the famous Barbarossa brothers, who spearheaded the repulsion of the Spanish, and, among other accomplishments, recaptured Algiers (in 1529) and established the city as an Ottoman *sanjak* (province).

These events occurred well before Reverend Ólafur's time, but the same underlying dynamics were still in play in the early seventeenth century: the Ottoman empire continued the struggle to dominate the Mediterranean and its environs, and, between 1609 and 1614, thousands of Spanish Moriscos—descendants of the Muslim population who had been made to convert to Christianity—were forcibly ejected from Spain, many settling in the Maghreb, fueling anti-European and anti-

7. Dar al-Islam, meaning "the house/abode of Islam," refers to that part of the world which is Muslim, i.e., in which Muslims may freely practice their religion.

Christian sentiment. There were, however, other forces at work as well.

The Maghreb was not a hermetically sealed area. There was constant traffic between Christians and Muslims, both peaceable and not. Using oared galleys rowed by slaves, Barbary corsairs had been attacking ships and raiding coastal settlements around the Mediterranean since the days of the Crusades, but by the seventeenth century they were also relying on European-style "round bottomed" sailing ships. It was such vessels—and the Europeans who knew how to navigate and sail them—that made possible long-distance expeditions like the one to Iceland.

European privateers had prospered for decades during the sixteenth century. Even when times were good, there had been a certain amount of defection—ships that, for whatever reasons, switched allegiances and began operating out of Maghrebi ports—but when the various conflicts between Spain, Britain, the Netherlands, and France wound down around the turn of that century, life as a privateer, particularly for British and Dutch privateers, became more and more problematic. Some gave it up and returned to more ordinary, peaceful pursuits. Many of those who did not found safe haven in Maghrebi ports. It has been estimated that from the latter part of the sixteenth century well into the middle of the seventeenth and beyond, over half the corsair *ru'asa* (plural of Arabic *ra'is*, meaning "captain") were Europeans, both ex-privateers wishing to continue in their lucrative profession, and captives who had "turned Turk," become Muslim, and worked their way up to positions of power. The home ports of these European ru'asa might have been in North Africa, but while in northern waters, their ships could put into European ports to refit and replenish their provisions, as long as they were careful to approach only those countries with which the Ottoman Porte or their home city had treaty relations. There are even stories that, during the mid-seventeenth century, such corsair ru'asa took control of Lundy, a small island in the Bristol Channel, and used it as a northern base of operations.

In short, the situation was not simple. Barbary corsairs were not just lone-wolf pirates nor just fanatical North African Muslim *jihadis*. Nor were they restricted to the Mediterranean. All this needs to be kept in mind in order for the details of the Tyrkjaránið to make sense.

In the letter in which Kláus Eyjólfsson chronicles the events of the Tyrkjaránið (see Letters section), he has this to say about its origins:

Some of those who escaped captivity maintain that two Lords of the Turkish empire made a bet with each other, one wagering against the other that it would not be possible to get even the smallest stone out of Iceland, much less a man. Because of this wager, the expedition was prepared and equipped, and twelve ships were sent to Iceland to capture as many people as possible and bring them back unharmed, for it is said that even one infant could fetch as much as three hundred *dalers* in Algeria.[8]

---

8. The "daler" mentioned here and in other parts of the text is the Danish *rigsdaler*, the major unit of seventeenth century Danish (and thus also Icelandic) currency. The rigdsaler was derived from the *thaler*, a coin widely recognized throughout Europe for several centuries. Over time, the term "thaler" morphed into the familiar English term today: dollar. We have, however, chosen to use "daler" instead of "dollar" throughout the text because modern readers might automatically think in terms of today's currency when seeing the familiar word, and the seventeenth century daler had a different role and a different value from today's dollar. For a discussion of seventeenth century currency, see Currencies and Distances in the Icelandic Background section of the Appendixes.

Chapter 1 of *The Turkish Raid Saga* adds the following: "With these pirate captains in their discussions was a Danish captive who had been a slave for a long time, although he was of the Christian faith.... This man saw a chance for himself to be set free from captivity and slavery by showing the pirates how to get there [to Iceland]."⁹

Whether there ever was any actual bet made between Turkish "lords" we will probably never know (unless some previously undiscovered document shows up). The notion of a Danish slave offering to pilot the corsair ships in return for his freedom is perfectly plausible, however.

Emanuel d'Aranda, a Flemish soldier/gentleman enslaved in Algiers from 1640 to 1642, gives an alternate version:

At my departure from Algiers, in the year 1642, a young man in Turkish habit came to me, having heard that I was a Dunkirk slave, and intended to pass through Madrid, and gave me a petition handsomely written in Latin, desiring me to present it to the ambassador of Denmark, then resident with the king of Spain.... It had happened some years since, said he, that an Iceland *renegado*,¹⁰ having been a long time abroad with the pirates of this city, without taking any prize, proposed to his captain, vexed that nothing fell in his way, to make towards Iceland, and, landing there, to take Icelanders, who suspected not that there were such barbarous people in the world. The proposal was liked by the captain, and the management of the enterprise was committed to that perfidious Icelander.... The Turks sent fifty soldiers ashore, who brought away about eight hundred

9. *The Turkish Raid Saga*, known as the *Tyrkjaráns-saga* in Icelandic, contains an account of the corsair raid on Iceland compiled from a variety of firsthand sources. It was written by Björn Jónsson in 1643, at the behest of Bishop Þorlákur Skúlason.

10. The term "renegado" was commonly used to describe a European Christian who had "turned Turk," i.e., who had renounced Christianity and become a Muslim. The term comes from the Spanish *renegado* ("renegade").

men, women, and children, and afterwards sold them in this city for slaves.[11]

Whatever the genesis of the raid might have been, the general consensus is that the Tyrkjaránið was organized by a Dutch renegado named Jan Janzoon, also known as Murat Reis the Younger.[12] Chapter 2 of *The Turkish Raid Saga* has this to say: "These [corsair] ships came in two groups to Iceland, and were from two cities in Barbari. I now want to talk first about the one ship, from the city which is named Kyle, which had on board three officers, the Admiral Amórað Reis, and the Captains Areif Reis and Beiram Reis."[13] This "Admiral Amórað Reis" is generally believed to be the Murat Reis credited with organizing the raid on Iceland. The common account of Murat Reis goes as follows.

Murat Reis was born Jan Janszoon (also sometimes spelled Jan Jansen, Jan Jansz) in Haarlem in about 1570. By around 1600 he was a participant of the Eighty Years' War (1568–1648, also known as the Dutch War of Independence), sailing as a privateer, with an official letter of marque, attacking Spanish vessels. Around 1618 he was taken captive by Barbary corsairs on the Canary Islands, "turned Turk," and became a corsair ra'is preying on European vessels. He also became the "grand admi-

11. This anecdote is in "Relation XLIII. Of the impious dutifullness of an Iseland-Slave," in *The history of Algiers and its slavery with many remarkable particularities of Africk, written by the Sieur Emanuel d'Aranda, sometime a slave there, English'd by John Davies.* We have modernized spelling, capitalization, and so on. See the Suggestions for Further Reading section for bibliographical details of this book. This passage seems to be the source of the erroneous figure of eight hundred Icelandic captives that one frequently encounters in descriptions of the Tyrkjaránið.

12. Murat Reis is also sometimes spelled Murat Rais, Murad Reis, Murad Rais, Morat Reis, Morat Rais. *Reis* in all its variant spellings is the Anglicization of the Arabic ra'is, "captain."

13. "Kyle" is Björn Jónsson's rendering of "Salé."

ral" of the independent "pirate" republic of Salé (on the Atlantic coast of what is now Morocco). Since, presumably, he knew northern waters, he led a series of raids there (including one on Baltimore, Ireland, in 1631, as well as the Icelandic raid in 1627). One (rather unlikely) version of the story has it that after a failed expedition in the winter of 1627, during which his vessel was nearly captured by a Spanish ship and he had to put into a Dutch port for repairs, Murat Reis devised the Iceland raid as a means of recouping his losses.

Whether the details of Murat Reis's story are historically accurate is not especially important for our purposes here. The story outlined above typifies the times perfectly. There were many such men—straddling the Christian and Muslim worlds—and one or another of them, or possibly several working together, must have organized the raid on Iceland. The crew, too, would have been mixed, a combination of Christian renegados, Ottoman janissaries (who functioned as "marines" on corsair ships), other Muslims, and Christian slaves serving as sailors.

It is not easy to sort out the exact details of the raid. Icelandic accounts say there were two separate corsair groups. One group, from Salé, in a single ship, attacked Grindavík and Bessastaðir in the southwest corner of the island. Another group, from Algiers, in three ships, attacked the southeastern coast and the Westman Islands. Accounts indicate that Murat Reis was the "admiral" in charge of the Grindavík raiders, but, if so, for a famously ruthless and successful corsair captain, he did not apparently achieve very much—or perhaps he was simply a very cautious and careful commander, willing to take what gains he could while running as little risk as possible. In any case, the Algiers expedition had more success. We have no clear idea of who was in charge of those Algiers ships, however, nor of what, exactly, the connection between the two sets of raiders might have been. Icelandic sources are not very reliable on this aspect of things, since Icelandic eyewitnesses and captives were hardly likely to be privy to the inner workings of the raid.

Father Pierre Dan, a Trinitarian friar who was in Algiers during 1634, wrote this about the Iceland raid:

In 1627 three ships from Algiers, led by a renegade German named Come Murat, were so bold as to go to the Denmark Sea where, making landfall on the island of Iceland, they took away numerous households, separating one person from the other, and making slaves of four hundred people whom they brought back [to Algiers].

Not to be outdone, in 1631, Morat Rays [Murat Reis], the Flemmish [Dutch] renegade, sailed to England, and from England to Ireland, where at night he put close to two hundred soldiers into small boats and descended upon a little hamlet, named Batinor [Baltimore], where they surprised some fishermen who lived on that isle. They took 237 people, men, women, and children, even those in the cradle. This done, they brought them to Algiers.[14]

Dan clearly believes that the Icelandic and the Irish raids were organized by two entirely different men. It is possible that Come Murat (the German renegado) could have been in charge of the three Algiers ships, while Murat Reis (the Dutch renegado) could have been in charge of the sole ship from Salé. There is, however, no way to determine this. We simply do not have the requisite supporting documents. As is the case with so many historical events, we will likely never know the true details. We do know one thing for certain: it was the Algerian contingent that took Reverend Ólafur and his family captive on the Westman Islands.

14. *Histoire de Barbarie et de ses corsairs, des royaumes, et des villes d'Alger, de Tunis, de Salé, et de Tripoli*, book 3, chapter 4, section 5. See the Suggestions for Further Reading section for bibliographical details of this book. The translation is our own.

CR

According to Icelandic sources, the story of the raid is as follows. Since Iceland was a Danish possession, the Danes typically sent warships every year to patrol Icelandic territorial waters. In 1627, however, the Danish crown was three months late in sending those ships. Iceland thus lacked the defenses it usually enjoyed, and the corsairs had no armed protective fleet to face. The convoy of warships did not leave Denmark that summer until July 20—the day after the last corsair ships sailed away from Iceland.

On June 20, the ship from Salé made first landfall at Grindavík, a trade and fishing port on Iceland's southwest shore. At Grindavík, the corsairs captured twelve to fifteen Icelanders, two Danish merchant ships, and around a dozen Danish men. From Grindavík, they sailed around the Reykjanes peninsula to Álftanes (close to present-day Reykjavík), where the Danish Governor of Iceland, Holgeir Rosenkrantz, had his residence at Bessastaðir. The largest corsair ship stranded, however, and it took a full day to get it afloat again. The day after that, the raiders departed, without attacking Bessastaðir, and sailed northwest towards Snæfellsjökull. Supposedly, after hearing a rumor of English warships in the waters about the West Fjords (Vestfirðir), they turned back to Salé, having taken a total of about thirty people and one Danish merchant ship.

On July 5, the Algiers ships made landfall at the Lón (near what is now Höfn) on Iceland's southeast coast. From there, they raided several areas, including Djúpivogur in the East Fjords (Austfirðir). Estimates are that they took over a hundred Icelanders and eighteen Danish people captive, and that they killed five or six people and wounded many more.

The two Algiers ships then sailed from the East Fjords

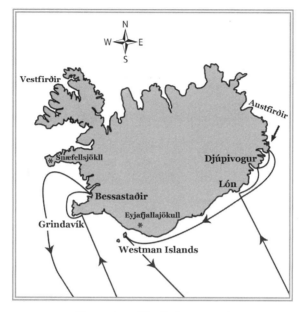

1. The routes of the Barbary corsairs

along the south coast, a long stretch of land where there are no harbors. A third ship joined them. All three ships came to Heimaey,[15] the largest of the Westman Islands and the only one permanently inhabited, on July 16.[16]

Off the coast near Eyjafjallajökull, the corsairs had captured

---

15. "Heimaey" is pronounced "*Hay*-mah-ay."

16. The corsairs seem to have known exactly what they were doing. Grindavík was one of Iceland's major towns. Bessastaðir was the seat of the Danish governor (who collected and held taxes to be shipped back to Denmark). Djúpivogur was the prominent Danish trading post on the southeast coast. Heimaey, also, boasted a prominent Danish trading post. All these were places likely to hold concentrations of people and wealth. The obvious inference here is that somebody aboard the corsair ships was very familiar with Iceland.

an English fishing vessel with a crew of nine men.[17] They promised the captain that they would allow him and his men to go
free if he showed them the best landing spot on the Westman
Islands. Among the English boat's crew was an Icelander who
agreed to show the raiders a way to land on Heimaey without
having to use the harbor, which was defended.

Using this alternate landing spot at Brimurð, some three
hundred raiders came ashore on the southeast corner of the island (see map 2 for locations on the island). They split into three
groups. The largest, over a hundred men, descended upon the
Danish merchant houses at the harbor. By that time, however,
the Danish factor, Lauritz Bagge, and the people with him had
escaped to the mainland in two small boats. When the raiders
realized that the inhabitants of the island were unarmed, they
split up into smaller groups of four to ten men, taking whatever
booty and captives they could find. They first imprisoned their
captives in the Danish merchant houses, and then loaded them
onboard their ships, which they brought into the harbor. They
burned the island's main church (the Landakirkja) and both
the island's vicarages—Ofanleiti, where Reverend Ólafur Egilsson and his people lived, and Kirkjubær, where Reverend Jón
Þorsteinsson (whom the raiders murdered) had lived.[18] The
raiders captured 242 men, women, and children on Heimaey
and killed somewhere between 30 and 40 people. After three
days of scouring the island, they left early on July 19 and set a
course for North Africa. Altogether, they took away from Iceland about 380 people.

17. Eyjafjallajökull (pronounced "Eh-ya-fiat-la-yer-kult") is the volcano on
Iceland's south coast that erupted in April 2010, sending a plume of volcanic ash
into the atmosphere and disrupting European air traffic.
18. The Þ in "Þorsteinsson" is the letter thorn (lower case, þ; upper case, Þ),
not found in the modern English alphabet. It represents the unvoiced "th" sound
in words like bath or worth.

2. The sea and land routes of the Barbary
Corsairs at Heimaey

The Westman Icelanders were sold into slavery in Algiers. They were, however, a relatively small addition to the slave population of that city. The Barbary corsair enterprise—attacking European shipping and settlements and taking booty and captives to ransom or enslave—was huge. Estimates are that from the beginning of the sixteenth to the end of the eighteenth centuries, perhaps as many as a million to a million and a quarter Europeans were enslaved in the Maghreb. There is some dispute over this estimate, but whatever the actual number may have been, it was high. In Reverend Ólafur's time, Algiers had a permanent population of something like twenty-five thousand slaves, which represented perhaps a quarter or more of the city's overall population. There was a fairly high turnover rate, however. Ransoms, escapes (rare but possible), outbreaks of plague, overwork, overcrowding, bad food, and utter despair all took their toll. A reasonable guess seems to be that the total attrition rate was about 25 percent. To maintain a stable slave population in a city like Algiers, therefore, something like six thousand new slaves had to be captured annually. Even if this is an overestimate—even if the actual number was, say, half as much—it was still a major undertaking.

In some ways, for some enslaved captives, life in a city like Algiers might offer more potential opportunities than had life in Europe. Algerian society was ethnically mixed and cosmopolitan, including such varied groups as its Ottoman rulers, Turkish janissaries, displaced Moriscos, Jewish merchants, Christian renegados, immigrants from all over the Islamic world, North African Berbers, and more. It was possible to "get ahead" in such a place through native intelligence, skill, or sheer brute perseverance in ways that were simply not conceivable in the more unyieldingly stratified societies of Europe. This should not blind us to the brutal realities of slavery, however. Slaves were property, to be used or abused as their owners saw fit. Captives with sufficient resources to pay a good ransom were normally spared the worst—it made a certain practical sense not to damage a potentially profitable commodity—but the daily existence of a typical slave could be grim and grueling. If they were lucky, those bought by private masters might end up as domestic servants. Those bought as public slaves typically ended up doing hard labor or wound up in the galleys, rowing one of the predatory corsair ships that hunted the Mediterranean. Galley servitude had a high mortality rate.

Because of the Islamic interdiction against owning Muslims as slaves, it was possible for an enslaved European to attain freedom by "turning Turk"—renouncing Christianity and becoming a Muslim. This was complicated, though. On the one hand, turning Turk could be seen as a transparent ploy on the part of the slave to escape his captivity, and it meant that the slave's owner lost his investment. On the other hand, converts to Islam were seen as triumphs, and slaves were actively encouraged, sometimes brutally, to convert.[19] Some slaves did become Muslims and successfully constructed new lives for themselves, especially those captured young. For many, though, the thought of renouncing their religion was too much, and they clung to their faith—hoping against hope they would be freed, for, unlike slaves in the Americas, a slave in the Maghreb could be set free at any time, as long as an acceptable ransom was paid. Slaves spent their days (years) yearning fervently to be ransomed. Those who could, wrote (or got somebody else to write) letters home imploring aid. Many were indeed ransomed, either by their families, their monarchs, or through the good graces of the Trinitarians, the Mercedarians,[20] or other groups devoted to ransoming captives. Many more were never ransomed, however, and ended their lives miserably.

19. There may be an element of propaganda in the stories of violent methods used to force Christians to convert. Joseph Pitts (in chapter IX of *A True and Faithful Account of the Religion and Manners of the Mohammetans ...*) writes, "It is usually reported ... that when any Christians are taken by the Algerines, they are put to extreme tortures, that so they may be thereby brought over to the Mahometan faith.... But I do assure the reader it is a very false report; for they [the Algerines] very seldom use such severities on that account.... They do not use [violence] to force any Christian to renounce his religion." See Auchterlonie's *Encountering Islam* and Vitkus' *Piracy, Slavery, and Redemption*, cited in the Suggestions for Further Reading section. Both works contain versions of Pitts's captivity narrative.

20. The Trinitarians (the Order of the Most Holy Trinity, founded in 1198) and the Mercedarians (the Order of the Blessed Virgin Mary of Mercy, founded in 1218) were the two main Catholic Redemptionist orders, whose mission was to ransom enslaved (Catholic) Christians.

Most of the Icelanders taken in the Tyrkjaránið vanished without a trace. Many must have succumbed to the deadly combination of sickness, overwork, and despair. A decade after the raid, when ransom arrangements were finally concluded, only thirty-four people were redeemed (twenty-six women and eight men), and only twenty-seven of that group ever made it back to Iceland.[21]

Though it is the drama of the corsair raid and of the brutal experience of Algiers that tends to stand out, *The Travels* is also filled with a wealth of social, political, economic, religious, and quotidian detail about Europe.

Reverend Ólafur left Algiers on September 20, 1627, bound for Copenhagen, where he hoped to raise ransom money for his family and, presumably, the other captive Icelanders. The journey took him a little over six months (he arrived in Copenhagen on March 28, 1628). He sailed from Algiers to Livorno, traveled on foot from Livorno, past Milan, northwards (in an abortive attempt to take an overland route to Copenhagen), then returned to Livorno and sailed from there to Genoa, from Genoa to Marseilles, from Marseilles to Holland, and then from Holland to Denmark and, finally, Copenhagen. After several months in Copenhagen, he returned to Iceland, arriving at the Westman Islands on July 6, 1628, slightly under a year since his capture the previous summer. On his return, the islanders greeted him, as he puts it, as if he "had been their own best friend returned again from death."

On the European leg of his journey, Reverend Ólafur was

---

21. A few Icelanders had been ransomed individually in the early years after the raid. Recently, it has been suggested that eight more might have been ransomed in 1645 (eighteen years after the raid) and brought to Copenhagen.

3. Reverend Ólafur Egilsson's travels

traveling through a world entirely new to him, and his out-
sider's observations of the places he visited and the customs
he witnessed—especially, perhaps, his Protestant (Lutheran)
views on Catholic practices—are fascinating and revealing.

There are two final points about Reverend Ólafur himself that
the reader ought to be aware of before turning to *The Travels.*
First, Reverend Ólafur was a man of his times. He attempted
to cope with personal tragedy in the only way he knew how:
through his Christian (Lutheran) faith. At the end of most
chapters, he links his narrative to quotations or references from
biblical scripture, and he concludes the book with a theological

discussion. For those interested in the history of religion, such scriptural referencing provides a fascinating and enlightening glimpse into early seventeenth century Protestantism. For the modern secular reader, however, the insistent focus on things biblical may seem a bit heavy-handed in spots. But one has to remember that *The Travels* was written nearly four hundred years ago, and that the role of religion in daily life has changed drastically during those centuries. In this respect, *The Travels* is a window into a past long forgotten by most of us.

The second point is that Reverend Ólafur was in his sixties when he underwent his ordeal. It is worth keeping this in mind when one contemplates the physical and emotional strains he had to endure.

*The Travels* is a fascinating work in many ways. It is one of the earliest travel books by a northern, post-Reformation Protestant writer describing both Islamic and Christian civilization in the seventeenth century, and it contains a wealth of detailed observations. It is also a moving story on the human level: we witness a devout man recounting a bitter personal tragedy, and, like others before and after him, struggling in his own way to reconcile such calamity with his understanding of God.

To give a clearer sense of the extraordinary events connected with the Tyrkjaránið, we have included not only the full text of Reverend Ólafur's narrative but also a series of letters, all but two written by Icelandic captives to their relatives back in Iceland. These letters describe, in sometimes vivid and haunting detail, both the events of the raid itself and the conditions in North Africa under which the enslaved Icelanders lived.

The combination of Reverend Ólafur's narrative and the accompanying letters provides an in-depth, firsthand view of seventeenth century Europe and the Maghreb equaled by few other works of the period. Until our translation, however, none of this had been available except to readers of seventeeth century Icelandic or eighteenth century Danish. We are pleased to offer *The Travels of Reverend Ólafur* now to the wider audience that an English edition allows, for it is a work that deserves a place in world literature.

---

OVERLEAF: Title page of the original Danish edition of *The Travels of Reverend Ólafur Egilsson*, published in 1741

# En kort

# Beretning

## Om

## De Tyrkiske Søe=Røveres

onde Medfart og Omgang, da de
kom til Island i Aaret 1627, og der bort=
toge over 300 Mennesker, ihielsloge mange, og paa
tyrannisk Maade ilde medhandlede dem.

Sammenskreven af

### Præsten Oluf Eigilssen

Fra Vest=Manøe,

Som tillige blev ført derfra til Algier, og 1628
kom tilbage igien.

Men nu af Islandsk oversat paa Dansk.

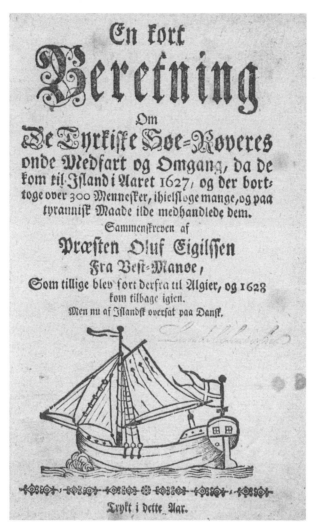

Trykt i dette Aar.

The text reads in Danish: En kort beretning om de tyrkiske Søerøveres onde medfart og omgang, da de kom til Island i året 1627 og der borttog over 300 mennesker, ihjelslog mange, og på tyranisk måde ilde medhandlede dem. Sammen-
skrevet af Præsten Oluf Eigilssen fra Vest Manøe, som tillige blev ført derfra til
Algier, og i 1628 kom tilbage igen. Men nu af islandsk oversat på dansk. (A brief
report on the Turkish raiders' wicked deeds when they descended upon Iceland in
the year 1627 and captured over 300 people, killed many, and terribly mistreated
all. Written by Reverend Ólafur Egilsson, from the Westman Islands, who also
was led away to Algiers, and returned in 1628. But now translated from the Icelandic into Danish.)

# THE
# TRAVELS OF
# REVEREND
# ÓLAFUR
# EGILSSON

## (Reisubók Séra Ólafs Egilssonar)

A book by the
Reverend Ólafur Egilsson,
who, with others, was captured on
the Westman Islands by Turkish
corsairs in the year of our Lord 1627
but returned to Iceland
in 1628

# Preface by the Copyist

REVEREND ÓLAFUR EGILSSON says that he was brought south to Africa to the Barbari,[1] to the place which is named Asser [Algiers], 500 miles further away than they who were captured in Grindavík,[2] and that he was again moved that same year; and he admonishes everyone to thank God and take care of themselves because what happened to him can also happen to others; and he writes an interesting Foreword about suffering, adversity, and misfortune in his travel book, which he said he was asked to compile to cover the period from the 16th of July 1627 till he came back to the Westman Islands on the 6th of July a year later.

This brief preface is from the Thott 514 manuscript. It was added more than a century after Reverend Ólafur originally penned *The Travels*. The foreword the copyist mentions has disappeared. See the Manuscript Sources in the Icelandic Background section of the Appendixes for a discussion of the various manuscript copies of *The Travels*.

1. "Barbari" is the form we have chosen to represent the seventeenth century Icelandic spelling of "Barbary" (Barbaríið), referring to the coast of North Africa.

2. The straight-line distance between Algiers and Salé (located on the Atlantic coast of modern-day Morocco), where the Grindavík captives were taken, is about 585 miles (942 kilometers), though the overland distance is about 800 miles (1,287 kilometers).

# CHAPTER I About almighty God's will ☙

IN THIS CHAPTER Reverend Ólafur Egilsson describes how, in the Old and New Testaments, warnings appeared before punishment came.[1]

1. This is all the text that remains of chapter I.

## CHAPTER II About signs and events ⟨⟩

REVEREND ÓLAFUR EGILSSON explains signs and events which happened here in Iceland, mainly in the Westman Islands, which were warnings for what happened later, but of which nobody took notice.[1]

1. This is all the text that remains of chapter II.

CHAPTER III About the preparations
that were put into effect when word
of the pirates was first heard ෨

WHEN NEWS OF the pirates' approach first reached Grindavík and southern Iceland, there were many grandiose words
and much fearless boasting, not in the least by the Danish authorities. A defensive rampart was built around the Danish
Merchant Houses on the Westman Islands, and ships prepared
for defense. The Danish boasted that the Icelanders would all
flee at the first sign of trouble.

Preparations stood like this until people heard that the pirates had gone away, and that they no longer posed any threat
to the Westman Islands.[1] After that, people became careless,
despite some warnings that had been given, and this went on
until the 16th of July, which was a Monday.[2] Then people saw

1. Reverend Ólafur is referring to the contingent of Salé corsairs who first
made landfall at Grindavík on June 20 and who, after successfully raiding Grindavík and unsuccessfully assailing Bessastaðir, set sail again for Salé three or four
days later.
2. Seventeenth century dates/days can be confusing because it is not always
clear from which calendar the date/day is derived. Europe used the Julian calendar (introduced by Julius Caesar in 45 BC) until the hind part of the sixteenth

View of the Danish houses on Heimaey

three ships early in the morning, off the south coast, and one of them was very huge. The ships headed towards Heimaey[3] but had a bad wind from the northwest and therefore were slow and had to make many a tack north and south all that day long.

When the three ships were first seen that morning, all the people were called to the Danish Merchant Houses for defense and strongly prohibited from leaving. They stayed there all that day until evening.

When night had come, however, the people went away be-

century, when the Gregorian calendar was officially adopted (Pope Gregory XIII decreed its adoption in a papal bull in 1582). Catholic countries changed over to this new calendar fairly quickly. Protestant counties did not. England, for example, only officially adopted the Gregorian calendar in 1752. Denmark adopted it in 1700. Since Iceland was a Danish possession in Reverend Ólafur's day, he would naturally use Julian dates. A quick check of a Gregorian calendar for 1627 shows that July 16 was a Friday. In the Julian calendar, however, it was a Monday.

3. Heimaey (pronounced "Hay-mah-ay") is the largest of the Westman Islands, and the only one permanently inhabited.

cause the Danish began to say that they thought the three ships must be part of the defensive force that had been sent to protect Iceland.[4] Then all the people went back to their homes and laid aside their preparations.

And so these servants of Satan, the father of all ungodliness, got their will.

Whatever happens, we are the Lord's.

4. Reverend Ólafur is likely referring here to the warships that the Danish Crown sent out each summer to patrol Icelandic waters. In the summer of 1627, the Danish fleet was late. See the Introduction for more detail on this.

# CHAPTER IV About the evil attacks and the methods used to capture some of the people ❧

THE NEXT DAY when the wind dropped, and while the people were still unprepared, the evil pirates lowered three boats overboard and very quickly put three hundred men into them and rushed ashore. In the boats were English pilots who had guided the pirates to a landing place, where none had ever before managed to come ashore.[1]

The pirates were ashore so suddenly that the people found it hard to escape them. They rushed with violent speed across the island, like hunting hounds, howling like wolves, and the weak women and children could not escape, especially on the farms above the lava, because the pirates had a shorter way there. Only a few of the people who were strongest, or had nothing to carry, or did not pay attention to anybody else, managed to avoid capture. I, with my weak group, was taken.

Some of my neighbors managed to escape quickly into

1. This was at Brimurð, on the southeast tip of Heimaey. See map 2.

the caves or down the cliffs, but many were seized and bound. Some were able to gain their freedom again, but who, exactly, I cannot tell, for I and my poor wife were amongst the first to be captured.

We struggled, along with others, for a long time until we were beaten and struck with the butts of their spears and had to give in. Most of those attacking us were English, and I have since wondered that they did not kill us all with their beatings.

We were then taken to the Danish Merchant Houses and there put into the new house, where there were already many other Icelanders imprisoned.

Of this, there is an example in Holy Scripture: Genesis 14. And the women of Media [Midian] with children: Numbers 21 [31:9].[2]

Whatever happens, we are the Lord's.

2. Reverend Ólafur sometimes gets his biblical references wrong, probably because he did not have a Bible at hand when he was writing. Bibles were rare in Iceland at this time. We have added some corrections (as here: Numbers 31:9 rather than 21). When he quotes the Bible verbatim, we have used the text from the King James edition.

CHAPTER V **About what honest people told me of how the pirates captured the Icelanders, and how some Icelanders were killed** ☙

WHAT FOLLOWS, I have heard from four men who were left behind when the pirates departed. These men were Oddur Pétursson, Bjarni Valdason, Magnús Egilsson, and Jón Snorrason. They saw what the pirates did, how people were treated, and how some of the Icelandic people were captured or killed. What follows are their honest statements.[1]

Three of these men were, with their wives and children, hidden in small caves in Fiskihellar[2] Mountain. But Oddur Pétursson was up on the slopes of the mountain named Háin[3] and was thereby the most able to see what happened.

The evil pirates divided themselves into three groups. The

---

1. Reverend Ólafur composed *The Travels* in Iceland after his return. He would have had ample opportunity to confer with people who had been eyewitnesses to the raid but managed to escape capture themselves.

2. "Fiskihellar" is pronounced "*Fisk*-ee-hetlar." See map 2 for its location.

3. "Háin" is pronounced "*How*-in." See map 2 for its location.

11

group which was the biggest (perhaps one hundred and fifty strong) went straight along to the Danish Merchant Houses and immediately attacked the houses. This was easy for them because the Danish had all fled half an hour earlier. The other two pirate groups quartered the island, capturing people wherever they found them, young and old, women and men and infants. The pirates chased after people in their houses, across the mountain slopes, in caves and holes, even in inaccessible places where the Icelandic folk could not go except very carefully. The pirates killed everybody who fought against them, and anybody who made the sign of the cross or named the name of Jesus.

The dead lay everywhere, though most of all by the Danish Merchant Houses. Four were shot to death in caves. Four others were lured from there and deceived by the Turkish pirates. The Reverend Pastor Jón was killed down by the seashore close to his home.

All this the four aforementioned men saw, though Oddur Pétursson looked closest at it because he had the best view of the Danish Houses, standing up there on the mountain Háin.

At this time, the wind turned to the east, so that the scoundrel pirates got all they could wish. As the prophet says: "You let them free so they should be slaughtered and saved them for killing." One of the Turkish ships, which had never reefed sail, took advantage of the changed wind to sail at once into the harbor, where it shot off three cannon. After that, one of their men jumped east to the rocks on the seashore with a captured Danish flag and waved the others in. The other ships soon came into the harbor because they knew now there was nothing further to worry about.

Oddur looked upon all of this from up on the Há, until the Landakirkja church stood in flames. Then he said that he fled into another place for his safety, and was there until Thursday morning.

What happened after that, none of the four men can say. So it falls upon me—upon whom great harm fell—to tell of what happened as truly as I know how.

Everything happens as the Lord wants: when we are judged, then are we punished by God, so that we are not lost eternally.

CHAPTER VI About how the people were treated as captives by the evil men and put into the Danish Merchant House, and then taken forth and placed onboard a ship ⌘

ON TUESDAY, as those of us already captured sat in the Danish Merchant House where we had been driven, the evil pirates gathered together everyone else whom they had taken, and in that crowd I saw my children. It was by now midday. The three houses where we were kept could no longer contain all the people, so the pirates ordered us to stand on the pavement in front of the houses, where we were surrounded by those evil men.

When I came out of the house and saw their commander, I went up to him with my poor wife and we fell on our knees in despair in front of him and his under-captain and begged for mercy, but our begging did no good. When I saw their headgear, I knew that these pirates were Turkish and that they must be intending to take us away to their land as slaves.

Then all those taken prisoner who were considered to be in acceptable condition were transferred hastily to the pirates' ship in two ten-oared boats. The Icelanders were ordered to row against a sharp easterly wind, and they were beaten and flogged with ropes. Then we were forced onto the pirates' biggest ship, which had lain there at anchor in the deeper part of the harbor and never come near shore. When the pirates on that ship saw us climb miserably aboard, they laughed. There were men on that ship already, in chains, who had been captured in the east of Iceland. We expected that we too would be put in chains, but this did not happen. Instead, we were given bread to eat and water to drink (though the water was bad), and the other prisoners were released from their chains and also given bread, which they ate ravenously because they had suffered from hunger until then. Then some of the evil pirates went back to the island to fetch more of those they had captured. Looking towards shore, we saw the Landakirkja church in flames.

A short time thereafter, I was called to the stern of the ship, and commanded by the pirate captain to sit down. At once, two of the Turks took my hands and bound them tightly together while others bound my feet. The captain then beat me, striking and kicking me along my back while I screamed helplessly with the pain of it. I do not know how many blows he gave me, but he beat me as hard as he could until I was too hoarse to scream any longer. Then a man was brought forward who spoke German.[1] He asked me if I knew about any money that might be anywhere. I said forcefully that I knew of none, and wanted only that they beat me to death quickly and have done. They left me

---

1. Though he never actually says so, Reverend Ólafur apparently understood, and possibly could speak, some German. This may help explain some of his choices in traveling companions and routes of travel later on in his journey across Europe.

alone then, raised me up, and ordered me back to the bow of the ship. I could hardly stand or walk, so badly had they hurt me. My fellow Icelanders had compassion for my poor plight, but the evil pirates just laughed.

God tests his people, and, as it is written: He wanted to humble you, to know what was in your heart. Deuteronomy 5 [Deuteronomy 8:2].

## CHAPTER VII About events in preparation for sailing ❧

IN THE AFTERNOON of that same day, the pirates came with more captives. They gave one man from the East Fjords his freedom, for he had a crippled hand. In the middle of the evening, we were taken belowdecks on the ship, where there were other prisoners, and given some food. We lay that night each where he was, as best we could find the space.

On Wednesday morning, the pirates brought still more people, and we saw great smoke from the Danish Houses, and they were said to be all afire in one great burning. It was then that I first heard the sorrowful news of the death of that man of God, Reverend Jón, and that his people were all taken.

For the whole of that day, the evil pirates were continually coming and going from the ship, and on each trip they came with more wretched people as prisoners.

But so that you, honest reader, should know the truth, I must say that after the people came aboard the ship at this time, the pirates did not annoy anyone except me, but behaved well towards them all, and were even kind to the children—though this does not make the story any happier.

Now, it may happen that you would like to know what these vile pirates looked like, both in personal appearance and in dress. Truly speaking, they are like other people: different in size and look, some small, some large, some black. Some are not of Turkish origin at all but are Christian people of other countries such as England, Germany, Denmark, or Norway. Those of this group who have not forsaken their religion dress after their own fashion but have to labor and are sometimes beaten as a reward.

The Turks themselves all dress the same, with red caps pointing upwards, the lower parts of which—some made of silk, some of other material—are wound like turbans. They wear long jackets, bound around the waist with a strip of cloth four fathoms in length,[1] and light linen trousers. Many wear no socks, but have red, yellow, and black shoes with iron-shod heels. The Turks all have black hair, and they shave their heads and their beards, except on the upper lip.[2] In truth, they are not a very wicked looking people. Rather, they are quiet and well-tempered in their manner—if it is possible to describe them like that. But the ones who have once been Christians and have forsaken their religion, although they dress like the Turks,

1. A fathom equals 6 feet (1.83 meters).

2. Reverend Ólafur's description of "Turkish" apparel matches well with that of Father Pierre Dan, the Trinitarian friar who was in Algiers in 1634: "They wear their shirts over their pants and cover themselves with a type of clothing they call a jacket, made in the form of a cassock out of cloth or silk, which is closed in front with large buttons of gold or silver, and which hangs a little below the knees.... They all shave their heads except for a small flake of hair they leave at the top, by which they believe their false prophet will lift them to paradise.... Many shave their beards, leaving only the moustache, which they let grow long. Their turban is a red wool cap which they wrap in folds of a fine white cotton cloth five or six yards in length.... Their shoes, shod with iron in a half-circle under the heel, are yellow leather, or red" (*Histoire de Barbarie*, book 2, relation 5, chapter 2).

are by far the worst of people, and cruelly brutal to Christians. It was they who bound those taken captive and wounded and killed people.

The most accurate reckoning of the number of Icelandic people killed is that there were thirty-four. There were two hundred and forty-two people captured in all, and, by Wednesday evening, all were aboard the Turkish ships.

Remember that suffering is part of this world and do not be discouraged. [Hebrews 12:5.]

Believe that we are the Lord's.

# CHAPTER VIII About our travel to the Barbari Coast and what happened during that voyage ◌

ON THURSDAY MORNING, the 19th of July, about mid-morning, the pirates weighed their anchors. These evil people made sail at the same time as the big ship which lay off eastwards. Then they saw the *Crab*—the ship they had captured from the Danish—come from land. When they had unreefed the sails, they shot off nine cannon and joined their little fleet of ships together. Then they set their course by Elliðaey Island and then southwards, and kept that course for three weeks, with the best, most direct fair wind they could wish for.[1]

When the poor Icelandic people saw their homeland disappearing behind them, there was much wailing and lamentation all that first day. When, finally, the wailing diminished, they tried to comfort each other in their plight with God's words, women as well as men, both young and old, because God had given these people true understanding about their salvation.

1. Elliðaey (pronounced "*Et*-leethe-ah-ay") is a small, uninhabited island a couple of miles (3.2 kilometers) northeast of Heimaey.

Praised should be the name of the Lord.

Though some people remained silent, many talked about the fate of others who had been led away into captivity and about how the Lord preserves his people in distress. For Him, nothing is impossible.

On the next Saturday thereafter, the 21st of July, people were fetched from one of the other Turkish ships and brought aboard the big one where I and my people were, among them the two Margréts and Jón Jónsson.[2] I and my wife and our children were taken apart from the other people and put in a place by ourselves and some cloth was given us to lie on. The pirates made a place for us to sleep every night with an old sail and a big tent which they had stolen from the Westman Islands. As it was dark down in the hold where they imprisoned us, lamps burned day and night.

They gave us all food at mealtimes. From the Westman Islands they had stolen a barrel of beer and one of mead. As long as these lasted, they were given us to drink. They had chopped up many of the wine and beer barrels in the Danish Merchant Houses and burned the rest. Most mornings, we got two bowls of spirit—of aqua vitae [brandy]. The Turks never drink anything other than water.

On the 30th of July, my poor wife gave birth, after the proper time, to a boy child who was named after the blessed Reverend Jón Þorsteinsson. God should always be thanked. I myself baptized the child as if we were back on land, but my heart was filled with grief.

When the pirates heard that a child had been born, and

2. The "two Margréts and Jón Jónsson" mentioned here are the wife (Margrét), the daughter (Margrét), and the son (Jón) of Reverend Jón Þorsteinsson, the pastor at Kirkjubær parish on the island of Heimaey who was murdered during the corsair raid. Jón Jónsson (Reverend Jón Þorsteinsson's son) is mentioned in the letter written by Jón Jónsson.

heard the child crying, they gathered in a flock. Two of them gave old shirts to wrap the child in.

Have pity upon me, friends, because the hand of God has touched me.

On that voyage, there was one of the pirates on our ship who washed himself normally every day in water. He was also washed by others during the month that we were travelling. The honest woman Margrét said that this pirate had killed her husband. All this washing could not make him clean, even though he might have held to the words of Moses, to wash clothes and bathe in water. [Exodus 19:10, 30:10.]

But we believe that we are the Lord's.

### CHAPTER IX About some difficulties that the Turks had on the voyage and about how they reacted ☙

AFTER A FEW DAYS of August had passed (it was the 5th), there came such a strong northeast wind that one ship was nearly wrecked, and that ship drifted away from the others. The evil pirates grew afraid, for they thought they would die of this storm. Close to midnight, such huge waves rose over our big ship that the large boat (which they call *slúffur*) was torn from its moorings on deck and driven against the lee gunwale by the sea, where it broke, and with it went one of the Christian pirates, who was Spanish. Another hurt his arm, but, even so, had to go up on the yardarm, from where he fell into the sea. I think he was German, because he cried out with uplifted arms and eyes: *"Hilf mir, Herr Gott!"* ["Help me, dear God!"]

The Christian captives were very peaceful, and many of them prayed with good words to God, readying themselves for death. But the evil pirates took the decision to slaughter a ram (a very fat one) as a sacrifice either to the Devil or to some one of their idols—I do not know which. They cut the ram into two pieces and threw a piece over each side of the ship, and the storm became calm within a few hours.[1]

During our month of travel, two or three old women died who had been taken captive in East Iceland. Their bodies were wrapped in old sailcloth, and they were quickly tossed overboard.

On the 9th of August, we came in sight of Hispanien [the Spanish/Portuguese coast]. There we encountered a fleet of six ships. The evil pirates became afraid of this fleet and began to arm themselves. So afraid were they that, as they took up their weapons, they shook like dogs coming out of cold water.

But it became apparent that the ships were Turkish, and similar in evil deeds to those who had captured us, for they were part of a fleet of twenty-seven ships that had left that place of evil people known as Asser fourteen days ago to rob and murder Christians.[2]

On the 11th day of August, the evil pirates who had captured us sailed through the narrow channel that men call Strát [the Strait of Gibraltar] which is four miles wide, between Spain and the Barbari Coast, near to Salé [on the coast of Morocco], the place to which the people from Grindavík were taken.[3]

1. Compare Reverend Ólafur's description of this sacrifice with that of Father Pierre Dan, the Trinitarian friar who was in Algiers in 1634: "When endangered by a storm, they take a sheep and cut it in half while it is still living.... This done, they take that half with the head attached and fling it into the sea on the right side of their ship, and the other on the left.... If, by chance, this first sheep has been needlessly sacrificed without the rough sea becoming calm, they take another sheep from among those they keep aboard the ship for this purpose, believing that the first had some defect which had prevented the success they expected.... If the thing once again fails, they repeat the sacrifice, sometimes employing up to ten or twelve sheep" (Histoire de Barbarie, book 3, chapter 6, section 2).

2. "Asser" is the term Reverend Ólafur uses when he refers to the city we now know as Algiers.

3. One would expect Reverend Ólafur to be using the Danish Sjællandsk

24

Captives being brought off the ships

During this part of the journey, the Turkish pirates were very afraid, because the Spanish catch them often here. But they got such a strong, favorable wind that they fairly flew along.

On the 16th or 17th of August we came to Asser, the place where our captors lived. Straight after the anchor had hit bottom, we captured people were put on land in a great hurry, and our sufferings—which God alone can redress—continued.

God controls all things according to His own will, and He tells us: thou shalt remember all the ways which the Lord thy God led thee. Deuteronomy 8 [Deuteronomy 8:2].

---

mile here as a unit of measurement (see Currencies and Distances in the Icelandic Background section of the Appendixes for a discussion of seventeenth century miles). The Sjællandsk mile equaled 6.92 statute miles (11.13 kilometers). The Strait of Gibraltar varies between 8 statute miles (13 kilometers) and 27 statute miles (43 kilometers) in width. If Reverend Ólafur does indeed have Sjællandsk miles in mind, 4 such miles would equal 27.6 statute miles, which corresponds quite well to the Strait's maximum width. "Strát" is pronounced "Strowt."

CHAPTER X **About how it went (to the best of my knowledge) for the good people who had been captured and were taken to that place [Algiers]** ℭℜ

WHEN THE POOR Icelandic people were put on land, such a huge crowd gathered that I think it was impossible to count their number. They did not come for any cruel purpose, but only to look at the poor captives. The Icelanders were separated from each other—friend from friend, children from their parents—and driven through the streets, from one house to another, to the marketplace where they were put up for auction as if they were sheep or cattle.

The people who had been captured in East Iceland were first offered for sale, the men being kept separate in some houses, the women in other houses. This went on until the 28th of August, by which time most of the East Iceland people were sold.[1]

1. Reverend Ólafur's narrative is a bit confusing. He makes it seem like the Icelanders were driven straight from the dock to the slave market. This was not

After that, the people from the Westman Islands were brought to the marketplace, which was a square built up of stones with seats encompassing it all around. The ground was paved with stones which appeared glossy—which I understand is because they were washed every day, as were the main houses, sometimes as much as three times a day. This marketplace was next to where their local king had his seat,[2] so that he would have the shortest way there, because, as I was told by those who had been there a long time (and were and are still Christians), their laws concerning the sharing out of captives were as follows.

First and foremost, the commander got to have whichever two of the captives he wanted. Then their king (if I may call him that) took every eighth man, every eighth woman, and every eighth child. When he had taken these, those people who remained were divided into two groups, one for the ship owners and one for the pirates themselves.

We poor Westman Islands people were taken to the marketplace in two groups, each of thirty. The Turks guarded each group in front and behind and counted heads at each street

---

the case. By his own account, it took eleven or twelve days to sell the hundred-odd Icelanders (and, presumably, the eighteen Danes) captured in the Eastfjords, and it was not until after this that the Westman Islanders were put up for sale. So they would have been housed for close to two weeks before being "driven through the streets, from one house to another, to the marketplace."

2. From other sources, we know that the Algiers slave market (the Batistan, also spelled Badistan and Badestan) was located on the Great Street of the Souk (Al-Souk al-Kabir), the long main street that ran transversely through the city. (See the Algiers and Salé section in the Appendixes for details on the layout of seventeenth century Algiers.) If Reverend Ólafur is right about the Batistan being located "next to where their local king had his seat," and if, by "king," he meant the Ottoman governor of the city (known variously as the bassa, pasha, beylebey, dey), then the Batistan was located close to the governor's residence, which we have called the Bassa's Palace. See the map of Algiers for the locations of the Al-Souk al-Kabir and the Bassa's Palace.

Captives being sold at the slave market—
the Batistan—in Algiers

corner because the inhabitants of that place will steal such captive people if ever they get the chance.

When we came to the marketplace, we were placed in a
circle, and everyone's hands and face were inspected. Then
the king chose from this group those whom he wanted (every
eighth, as I mentioned earlier). His first choice amongst the
boys was my own poor son, eleven years old, whom I will never
forget as long as I live because of the depth of his understanding. When he was taken from me, I asked him in God's name
not to forsake his faith nor forget his catechism. He said with
great grief, "I will not, my father! They can treat my body as
they will, but my soul I shall keep for my good God."

I have to say with Job: What is my strength, that I should
hope? (Job 6:11). Were one to try to weigh my misery and suffering altogether on a scale, they would be heavier than all the
sand in the sea.

The other Icelanders were moved from there to another place, and one of the Turks led two groups of ten around one stone column with loud screaming which I did not understand.[3] I and my wife and our two younger children, a one-year-old and a one-month-old, were taken from that place up to the king's hall, and there we sat with the children in our arms for two hours.[4] From there, we were then taken to the king's prison, where we spent that night.[5] From that time on, I do not know what became of the rest of the Icelandic people.

Ah! I would like to comfort and strengthen the people with my words, but I cannot. And whether I speak of such things or not, my suffering does not lessen. [c.f. Job 16:5, 6.]

Whatever happens, we are the Lord's.

3. Father Pierre Dan, the Trinitarian friar who was in Algiers in 1634, describes the sale of captives as follows: "Recently taken captives are brought out of the prison where they are kept under guard and brought to the Batistan.... There are brokers, like horse dealers, who, well versed in this business, walk beside the captives to the market, loudly shouting that they are for sale to whoever wants to buy them" (*Histoire de Barbarie*, book 5, chapter 2, section 1). Something of this sort is likely what Reverend Ólafur witnessed.

4. The Bassa's Palace.

5. The Great Bagnio. For details of this slave prison, see the Algiers and Salé section of the Appendixes.

## CHAPTER XI  About what happened to me and my family thereafter ⟨⟩

THE NEXT DAY, around midday, there came two captains, one German and one Norwegian, who also were imprisoned, who said they were supposed to fetch us. Carrying the young children, my wife and I followed them for a long distance through many streets until we came into the house of one of the Turkish chieftains.[1] At once, the younger child was given clothes and a cradle. Also, my wife was given cloth after their custom, and we were given food, though I was not allowed to eat with her.

To tell the truth, we captives were given ample food: evenings and mornings, we had bread warm from the oven and good porridge groats with fat put into it, and as much as we could want of apples and grapes. What was left in the evening of the bread was given to the horses in the morning, but the porridge was either thrown over the wall or—if I may say so— down into the privy. Nothing else was given us to drink other than lukewarm, brackish water.

1. It is difficult to determine who this "Turkish chieftain" was. He might have been Ali Pegelin, from whom Reverend Ólafur's wife was eventually ransomed. See the Icelandic Background section of the Appendixes.

Straight after the meal at this chieftain's house, I was taken away to another house where I had to wander alone all that day until night, when those who lived there came home. They were soldiers of the chieftain in whose house my wife and children were kept. I stayed in that place for three or four days. Thereafter I was taken a long way from there to a house where two men from the Westman Islands were already kept, Jesper Christiensson and Jón Þorsteinsson, a carpenter. We all three were kept there, as if in prison, and watched.

Two or three days later, I was brought in front of some of the Turks of the highest rank (apart from the King) and by them commanded to go and seek money of my gracious sovereign, King Kristján [Christian] of Denmark, to ransom my wife and my children (who were with their mother).[2] The Turks demanded a total of twelve hundred dalers, which they call *Stück von achten*.[3] Upon this, I had to kiss their hands.

Then I was returned to the same house to which I had

2. Reverend Ólafur only mentions ransom for his wife and children. It is likely, though, that his captors intended him to procure ransoms for the other Icelanders as well. Liberating Reverend Ólafur made a certain financial sense: given his age, he was not likely to last very long at slave labor, and so would not fetch a very high price at the slave market (the Batistan). The ransom money he could procure would more than offset the loss of his sale. Sending him off like this was a risk, but one his captors clearly felt worth taking.

3. The "daler" mentioned here and in other parts of the text is the Danish rigsdaler. Stück von achten is German for "pieces of eight," the famous Spanish silver coin of pirate legend. The German term is used in the Icelandic manuscript. Whether this was Reverend Ólafur's original choice of words or a copyist's is difficult to determine. The Spanish name for this coin was *real de a ocho* (*real* derives from "royal," so literally, "royal of eight") or *peso de a ocho* ("piece of eight," also known simply as the *peso*). The real de a ocho was a standard coin of internationally recognized value, equivalent in worth to a number of standard coins from other countries, including the rigsdaler. For a discussion of seventeenth century currency, see Currencies and Distances in the Icelandic Background section of the Appendixes. It is difficult to sort out precisely the relative buying power of the currencies mentioned in *The Travels*, but 1,200 dalers/Stück von achten/reales de a ocho was a great deal of money.

Algiers (Asser) in the seventeenth century

originally been brought, though I could walk freely there now within the confines of the wall—which I and Jesper did.[4] But my wife and children I could not visit, except very seldom, even though I very much wanted to see them.

Oh misery upon misery! I want to say, as did David: The Lord will lift up my head and smite the enemies that surround me. [Psalms 3:4 and 110:7?]

4. It is not clear what "wall" Reverend Ólafur may be referring to here (or earlier, when he says old porridge was thrown "over the wall"). Algiers was a walled city, so one would expect that in this passage he means he and Jesper Christiensson had been granted a certain amount of freedom to roam the city, as long as they remained inside the protective wall that encircled it. In the next chapter (chapter XII), however, he remarks, "The town is without a wall as far as I saw, except on that part which is along the seashore." Perhaps he is referring here to that wall "along the seashore," but perhaps not; it is simply not possible to tell from the text. See note 4 in chapter XII for a further discussion of his observation about the Algiers city wall. For a detailed description of the wall itself, see the Algiers and Salé section of the Appendixes.

CHAPTER XII **About the remarkable things I saw and about the town [Algiers] itself** ❦

WHAT I SAW IN that place of evil people is difficult for me to describe because I was so disoriented and grief-stricken at that time.

The first thing that we captives met on the streets when we came ashore were the donkeys, heavily laden. These animals are small by our standards, no bigger than a two-year-old mare, but they are very strong for carrying things. They have ears almost an ell long.[1] Their tails are thinner than horses' tails, and their coats are patchy, like thin beards here and there. They walk with a feeding basket on their mouths, tethered by a string band slipped behind their ears, in which is the bread that they eat while walking. This goes on day after day.

I saw no carriages used for work in that place. There were

1. The "Hanse Town ell," used generally in Iceland from the beginning of the sixteenth century until 1776, was 21 1/11 inches (approximately 53.5 centimeters). Reverend Ólafur probably had this measurement, or something very like it, in mind.

many horses with feed baskets filled with bread. These horses were very thin. Most of them pulled the quern to grind meal.

In that town, I also saw five camels, which are strong and enormous. I could hardly reach up to their backs when they had their saddles on—which are normally kept on them. It is my opinion that each of these animals can carry as much as four or five horses. They are all pale or fawn-colored, with a dark stripe down their backs. In some ways they resemble cattle, especially about their legs and feet, which are cloven. They have a humped back, very long necks, and smallish ears almost like those of a horse. Their heads are very ugly, and they have lips like a bull's. They also carry a feed basket of bread hung from their mouths. These animals are very slow. When they are whipped about their hind legs, they do not react in any way.

I also saw a dwarf man there and a dwarf woman, because they are so common in that town. He looked to me to be less than two ells tall, and she one-and-a-half ells tall. He had a short trunk and was long-legged with long arms reaching almost down to his knees. He was black as pitch with a big head. But she was astonishingly fat, with short, fat legs and a long trunk. I also saw birds of many different types and colors and behaviors. And I saw a peacock and many other sorts of birds in an aviary.

Now about the town itself, even though I do not much like to talk about it. I want to explain that it is white as chalk from limestone that is boiled in big iron kettles, under each of which fire burns in four places. The town is built up to a mountain. It is very narrow at the upper end near the top of the mountain, and very long and very wide at the sea.[2] I believe it to be at least

2. Reverend Ólafur's description of Algiers agrees well with other contemporary descriptions. Here, for instance, is a portrayal of the city from chapter 1 of Joseph Pitts's *A Faithful Account of the Religion and Manners of the Mahometans*

Algiers, showing the city rising up out of the sea

one *þingmannaleið* wide.[3] The town is without a wall as far as I saw, except on that part which is along the seashore.[4]

---

… *with an Account of the Author's being taken Captive*: "As to the city of Algier, it is situated on the side of a hill, and its Walls are adjoining to the Sea. The tops of the Houses are all over white, being flat and covered with Lime and Sand…. The upper part of the Town is not so broad as the lower, and therefore at Sea it looks like the Topsail of a Ship." See the Auchterlonie (*Encountering Islam*) or Vitkus (*Piracy, Slavery, and Redemption*) entries in the Suggestions for Further Reading section. Both works contain versions of Pitts' captivity narrative. For further descriptions of Algiers, see the Algiers and Salé section of the Appendixes.

3. The þingmannaleið (literally: "parliament man's way") was a traditional Icelandic unit of distance equal to approximately 23.5 miles (37.5 kilometers). It represented the distance a *þingmann* (a representative of the *Þing*, the Icelandic parliament) could travel in one day on horseback. Reverend Ólafur (or perhaps the copyist) is obviously mistaken here. The Algiers harbor front was certainly not 23.5 miles across.

4. This observation directly contradicts the accounts of other captives from this period who all agree that Algiers was a walled city. Perhaps the explanation

Each house is open at the top, and there are small, narrow rooms where people sleep. The windows have nothing other than iron grating in them. Because of the great heat which is there from the sun, men and women go almost without clothes.

Because the sun is always high in the sky, the land grows two crops during the year, and all the fruits of the earth—corn, grapes, grain (groats)—grow like this. The grass is never cut, and sheep and cattle are never put into houses because there is no winter there, never any frost or snow at any time the whole year round.[5] The sheep, which are both big and very fat, lamb two times a year. There are no barren or gelded sheep. In one day, Jesper and I saw 100 rams, with tails hanging nearly down to the ground.

Many there are who look fair and embellish themselves in order to better carry through their evil business, as David says.

Whatever happens, we are the Lord's.

---

is that Reverend Ólafur was there for only about a month (August 16/17 to September 20) and only saw the inner part of the city and the harbor front. Or perhaps, as he puts it himself, he was "so disoriented and grief-stricken at that time" that his observations are just not accurate. His description of the city is certainly piecemeal and seems to reflect the observations of a bewildered man catching momentary glimpses of things as he is moved about. For a detailed description of the Algiers city wall, drawn from contemporary seventeenth century accounts, see the Algiers and Salé section of the Appendixes.

5. Seventeenth century Icelanders slaughtered much of their livestock (cows and sheep) in the fall. Those they did not slaughter they housed in special buildings, often connected to their homes, during the winter. It was the best way to ensure the animals survived until spring came.

36

CHAPTER XIII **About the dress of the people and how their plates and drinking cups were in that place** ℭℛ

AS FOR PEOPLE'S CLOTHES, as I have said earlier, those who came to this land as Christians kept to their own manner of dress. The Turks say that in that place there are 9,000 Christian people who have been there for a long time.[1]

The Turkish women, firstly, wear very good dresses with many folds and pleats around the waist. These dresses are made of silk, of the finest weave which I think exists in the world. They are not open, except at the neck. Also, the women wear linen trousers down to their shoes, attaching one end of the cuffs to their instep and the other to their heels. They wear skullcaps made of linen, which are neat and handily made, and a mantle which is made either of circular-woven linen or other valuable weaving. When they go outside, they wrap the lap of the mantle around their face, so that, when they walk on the

---

1. One presumes that Reverend Ólafur is referring here to the population of European renegados in Algiers. He might be referring to slaves, though, or to both. It is not clear.

Maghrebi attire in the seventeenth century

streets, nobody knows them. But indoors, they wear good plain clothes without folds, though they wear linen trousers. The Christian women are dressed in a similar way, except that they do not wear trousers.

In that place, dishware is all made of either clay or copper. Dishes and washbasins are of tinned copper, but the drinking cups are all made of clay and have clay necks. Everyone has the same sort of drinking cups, both the Turks and the prisoners. In that place, they drink only warm, brackish water, which in many places is brought into the houses.

Most people in that place sleep on the floor without a mattress, but place thick blankets beneath and on top of them—though I had no experience of these. There were no storage chests to be seen and no barrels, where I was, and no tables or benches. They do not use knives when eating, and, as far as I could see, there were no spoons except those made of wood. There was no iron on the doors except for hinges. Most houses had swinging doors. When food is eaten, people sit straight-legged on the floor.

During the time that we three Icelanders were in that house, Jesper Christiensson and I felt unwell, but Jón Þorsteinsson became truly sick. Then my honest wife was allowed to visit me, but not to stay there very long. Ah! Lord, our transgressions deserve punishment, but you help us for your name's sake.

During that time, I was barefoot and had no shoes. Then God awakened one French man who had been there for a long time. That man gave me new shoes and also a liter of aqua vitae [brandy]. At the time I was ill, he gave me some homespun woolen cloth three ells in length. And that same man told me that many Icelandic people were lying sick and dying all around the town, which did not make us happy. He also told me that in the Christian cemetery there were already thirty-one buried. The Icelanders could not endure the terrible heat of that place.

That same French man also told me that a girl who had been my servant, who was very good looking, had been sold—first for 700 dalers, but then a rich man came from Jerusalem, thirty-eight miles to the northeast, and paid 1,000 dalers for her and took her back with him to Jerusalem where he gave her to a Christian man.[2] In that place, Christian men cannot have

2. Reverend Ólafur seems to have little idea of the geography involved here, since Jerusalem is vastly more than "thirty-eight miles" from Algiers, regardless of the distance one of his "miles" might actually represent. One manuscript version of *The Travels* puts this distance at 300 miles, but even this is far from accurate.

intercourse with Turkish women, nor Turkish men with Christian women. Otherwise, they lose their lives.

About such things I do not have need to write further, except to say that I witnessed these things and that they are truth. And since we are all bound to pray for each other, then do not forget, good Christian people, to pray for our captured kinsmen so that God will bless them and maintain them in their Christian belief, young as well as old, until their deaths, because it is God's good will that we surrender ourselves to His mercy, which has no end, but is renewed every morning. [Lamentations 2:22–23.]

---

The actual distance is about 2,500 miles (4,000 kilometers), and the direction is almost due east, not northeast. It is possible that Reverend Ólafur had a clearer sense of the distance than it appears, and that the copyists who later reproduced his original manuscript mistook the measurement.

CHAPTER XIV **About how I was driven from Algiers and how things went on my miserable travels** ∝

ON THE 20TH DAY of September, I was called from the house where I was imprisoned and taken to the house where my wife and babies were.[1] I begged with all humbleness and prayer of the captors who came to fetch me that I might be allowed to greet my wife and children (all of whom were already very sick). I was hardly allowed ten words with them, however, and then my captors callously pulled me away. Oh, oh, distress on distress:

> To lose both babies and wife
> makes one despair,
> but the returns into eternal life
> all separations repair.

Now, in the name of Jesus, the Lord says: "I am the one who made thee, and formed thee from the womb, and I will pour my

---

1. In this chapter, Reverend Ólafur is leaving for Denmark to try to raise money from the Danish monarchy to ransom his wife and children, and, presumably, the other Icelandic captives.

spirit upon thy seed and my blessings on thine offspring. Be not afraid." (Isaiah 44:2–3.)

After this painful meeting with my family, I was taken to the street where the official who was to issue me a safe-conduct lived. This safe-conduct, written in many languages, I was to give to any Turkish pirates who might capture a ship on which I was a passenger. The document explained that I should neither be killed nor interfered with because I was acting as a messenger. I still have this document and have shown it to several people, including the archbishop of Copenhagen.[2]

In order to receive this safe-conduct, I had to kiss the pirates' hands again. That same day, I was put aboard an Italian ship.

On this voyage I suffered great hardship and distress, and at one point, for lack of proper food and water, I was reduced to drinking water that a lion, a bear, an ostrich, and some monkeys and poultry had drunk from and befouled.[3] Even so, I was glad, so thirsty was I.

After we had been at sea for some time, we saw a Turkish ship which followed us for two days but did not catch us. The "friendship" between the Italians and the Turks is such that when they have completed trading with one another and

2. Technically speaking, there was no archbishop of Copenhagen after the Reformation. It is likely that this is a copyist's error, and Reverend Ólafur meant the Sjálandsbiskup (the bishop of Sjælland, i.e., Zealand, the island on which Copenhagen is located). The Sjálandsbiskup was the leader of the Danish church, and so of the Icelandic church as well. If it was this man, he was Hans Poulson Resen, who was bishop from 1615 until his death in 1638. This is almost certainly the "Doctor Hans Resen" with whom Reverend Ólafur dined in Copenhagen (see chapter XXIV).

3. Menageries were quite common in early modern Europe, and the list of standard animals in the collections included lions, leopards, bears, monkeys, ostriches, and camels. All of these came from Africa—the Atlas bear and the Barbary (also known as the Atlas or Nubian) lion from North Africa. It is possible Reverend Ólafur happened to be aboard a ship transporting several such animals to a European collector. One wishes he had spent a few more sentences explaining this tantalizing situation.

42

are one mile out from the harbor, they will set upon and kill each other remorselessly.

A week into this voyage, the sailing master lost his way (though he was a man who never helped very much, in my judgment).[4] Then we saw land on the port side, and because the sea was very calm, we dropped anchor, put a boat over the side, and rowed towards the shore.

I went with those going ashore because I did not dare to remain on the ship when my companion[5] went to the land because there were many sorts of foreign people aboard. There were seven Italians, four Jews (who sometimes gave us crumbs of bread), and also four English, three Spanish, and five French. Of the French I was particularly afraid because they constantly cast sour looks towards me and the five Germans (including my companion).

When we drew near the shore, we found that we could not come to the land except on a kind of skerry formed by rocks which had fallen from the steep cliff that formed the shoreline. As we drew near land, some people appeared on the skerry and threatened us. We assured them that all we wanted was to have some water, only four small hogsheads of it, but they refused to listen. The boat's crew asked what the name of this country was, and the people said it was called Sardinia.

As we lay-to there along the stones of the skerry, unable to

4. The Icelandic word here is *stýrimaður*, literally "steersman," which we have rendered as "sailing master." Reverend Ólafur is likely referring to the ship's pilot—that is, the man responsible for guiding the ship. In the seventeenth century, nautical charts were both less available and less accurate than today, and sailing vessels relied on such pilots, who made use of their personal knowledge of the area to act as navigators. This pilot appears to have gotten lost, hence Reverend Ólafur's low opinion of his abilities.

5. This is the first mention of any such "companion." He was Jacob Suarj, from Hamburg, and he, too, had been captured by the "Turks." Reverend Ólafur discusses him (briefly) in the next chapter.

land because of the people preventing us, a gale sprang up. We could not move, and we were stranded there for two days and a night with neither food nor drink. The boat's crew was very afraid about the ship because the weather had turned against us. But when the weather fell calm once more, we rowed straight out to the ship, which lay at anchor unharmed. Once aboard again, we had a good meal, but there was still little to drink.

A few days thereafter, we came to that island which is named Malta, where Saint Paul stayed for a while. Several days later we drew near Italy, where the ship's captain lived, and made harbor at a place named Legor [Livorno].[6] There, everybody had to wait on the ship for six days; no one could set foot on land until he had been examined by the master surgeon in charge.[7] The crew's wives, who lived there, could see their husbands, and talk with them, but could not come close to them.

One of the Italians gave me wine to drink and apples and cheese to eat, and this would have made me hope for better things to come except that it did not last. I can say as Job said: God's spirit has made me part of life. I am truly the Lord's. [Job 33:4.]

6. A sailing route from Algiers to Livorno that goes via Sardinia and then the island of Malta seems excessively roundabout. There are far more straightforward, quicker routes. Given Reverend Ólafur's lack of geographic knowledge of this part of the world, it is likely that he has this wrong, and that whatever island he may have sailed past, it was not Malta. On the other hand, prevailing winds and currents may have dictated this course, and Reverend Ólafur claims the ship's pilot (the "sailing master") lost his way. Rather than try to second guess him, in map 3 we have plotted the course he outlines and extended it from Malta north through the strait between Sicily and the "toe" of Italy, and so on to Livorno—an unlikely route, admittedly, but one that at least fits with his narrative.

7. The Livorno authorities were likely worried about bubonic plague (the "Black Death"). Intermittent eruptions of plague ravaged Algiers throughout the seventeenth century. One particularly devastating outbreak in 1620–21 is estimated to have killed upward of fifty thousand people. This event would surely have been in the minds of the Livorno port authorities. Such fears of infection were well founded. Northern and central Italy suffered a major plague epidemic only a few years after this (1629–31), in which nearly three hundred thousand people died.

# CHAPTER XV About what went on in that place [Livorno], good and bad, and about my journey to Germany ℂℛ

ON THE 11TH OF OCTOBER, we people aboard the ship were called to land. Each and every man was brought into a long house, some distance from the town, which had been built to provide a place to inspect people to see whether they were pestilence free,[1] and to determine if they had any other diseases.

When we arrived there, the master surgeon of this place came and ordered us to take our clothes off. When we had done this, he examined everyone under the arms and down to the groin, women as well as men. When this was over, then the people could enter the town. I went with the others, but with great grief and sorrow, for I could expect no help in this place except from God.

When I came into the town, to my good fortune, the English who had come with me from the Barbari invited me to

---

1. That is, not infected with the plague.

their table and paid for my food and drink (which was seven coins), and then arranged for me a room in a house belonging to a Norwegian man who lived in the town. That same man gave me food the day after, which was the 12th of October. The day after that, the 13th of October, I did not get anything to eat— wet or dry, as people used to say—but I was allowed to stay in that house.

But then my hardship was such that, in the name of God, I begged help of some of the merchants in the town, who were German and also English. They gave me five dalers or almost six, all in silver or gold, in small coins. I did not know this currency and so had to write things down.

We receive mercy from our fellow men through God's working.

The Norwegian man gave me ink and paper and helped me in many things. He boarded me free of charge, although I at last paid some back. With the money I had got, I wanted to travel with my travel partner, the German from Hamburg, whose name was Jacob Suarj.[2] This man, whom the Turks had captured in the springtime (before mid-May), had both wife and children in Hamburg. He had got no money at all in the town and was therefore totally helpless. I offered to share with him, for I did not know the currency nor the road I must take.

We traveled for four days and passed by that big place called Fenedíborg [Venice]. This town is enormous, and the larger part of it is on the sea rather than the land. Where we walked past the town, the city had a triple wall which was im-

2. Reverend Ólafur gives us few details about Jacob Suarj. He did not escape from Algiers—for no escaped slave could leave the city onboard a ship like a normal passenger—so he was either ransomed or (less likely) sent on a quest for ransom money, like Reverend Ólafur. The fact that Reverend Ólafur understood, and spoke, some German and so could converse with Suarj may explain, in part, why he chose the man as a traveling companion.

mensely tall to see.[3] It is said to be fourteen miles in circumference, which is four and a half þingmannaleið.[4] The sea, which there reaches into the land, is called Fenedíbotnar.

3. It seems that Reverend Ólafur misunderstood (or perhaps was even misled by) the local people with whom he interacted, and that he mistook Milan for Venice. Seventeenth century Venice had no fortifications corresponding to his description of "a triple wall which was immensely tall to see." Milan, however, did have such a wall. The Milan city walls consisted of three separate projects, the first built in Roman times, the second during the Middle Ages, the third (the Mura Spagnole, or Spanish Walls) during the middle of the sixteenth century by the Spanish Habsburg rulers of the city. The Spanish Walls formed a massive rampart 15 feet (4.6 meters) or more in height, studded with bastions and a dozen or so large *porti* (gateways), stretching for about 7 miles (11 kilometers) around the city. In the 1620s it would have been not much more than half a century old, and still in very solid shape, and it would no doubt have looked extremely impressive to a rural Icelander. The Spanish Wall was also encircled by a moat, which Reverend Ólafur could conceivably have mistaken for an arm of the sea ("The sea, which there reaches into the land …"). It should be remembered that Reverend Ólafur had only a limited ability to converse with those around him (he may have understood and spoken some German, but there is no indication he understood any Italian), he had never before traveled outside Iceland, except possibly to Denmark, and he had no real geographical knowledge of Europe. His confusing Milan with Venice is therefore quite plausible.

4. As noted earlier, a Þingmannaleið equals approximately 23.5 miles (37.5 kilometers). By this reckoning, the city would be about 106 statute miles (169 kilometers) in circumference (23.5 x 4.5 = 105.75). If Reverend Ólafur is referring to Venice here, this measurement is off by a factor of 10, since seventeenth century Venice was, at most, well under 10 miles (16 kilometers) in circumference. *Cook's Handbook to Venice* (1874), for instance, states: "Venice is seven miles in circumference, and is divided into two unequal halves by the Grand Canal." The nineteenth century city was hardly likely to be smaller than the seventeenth century one. If Reverend Ólafur is referring to Milan, he is equally far off, since seventeenth century Milan was not very much larger than Venice. (*Cook's Handbook to Northern Italy* (1881) states: "the circumference of the city [Milan]—which in shape resembles a hexagon—is about eight miles."). Given his figures, Reverend Ólafur's "mile" would equal 7.5 statute miles (12 kilometers) (23.5 x 4.5 ÷ 14 = 7.5). One would expect him to use the Danish Sjællandsk mile here as a unit of measurement (see Currencies and Distances in the Icelandic Background section of the Appendixes for a discussion of seventeenth century miles). The Sjællandsk mile equaled 6.92 statute miles (11.13 kilometers), which is close enough to his reckoning here to at least make sense. How he could have imagined these cities to be more than 100

We passed that mountain which is named Baldach where, it is said in the old story, Þorbjörg the Stout lived.[5] And then we came a very short distance into High Germany, a one-day walk.[6] We stopped and passed the night in the home of an old widow, who asked us where we had come from and where we wanted to go. When she heard our answers, she begged us for

miles (160 kilometers) in circumference is another matter. It is difficult to assess the accuracy of his measurements and observations, and even more difficult to ascertain how much of the confusion might be due to misperception or misunderstanding on his part and how much due to copyists' errors.

5. The "old story" Reverend Ólafur mentions is the *Jarlmanna Saga*, which features a giantess named Þorbjörg who lives on Baldach Mountain in Serkland (the Norse name for the Abbasid Caliphate, centered in Baghdad). Any mountain Reverend Ólafur saw would not, of course, have been located in what is now modern-day Iraq. It seems likely that what he saw was Monte Baldo—a mountain range in the Italian Alps reaching a maximum height of about 7,200 feet (2,200 meters), located just east of Lago di Garda (Lake Garda)—and that he conflated the two names—Baldach/Baldo. Since Roman times, one of the principal routes connecting northern Italy with what is now Austria/Germany has been the Passo del Brennero (the Brenner Pass), which cuts through the Alps across the modern border between Italy and Austria. The main road leading northward out of Italy toward the Passo del Brennero runs just east of Monte Baldo. The country through which Reverend Ólafur traveled would have been part of the Venetian Republic, which at that time contained vastly more territory than just the city itself, incorporating a broad swath of country extending from the Adriatic coast northward to Lago di Garda (a distance of nearly 125 miles/200 kilometers) and including such cities/towns as Padua, Vicenza, Verona, and Bergamo. The border with the Holy Roman Empire lay not far north of Monte Baldo. It makes sense that Reverend Ólafur and his companion, traveling on foot as they were, would take this route to the Passo del Brennero in their attempt to reach Germany, and that Reverend Ólafur would thus see Monte Baldo along the way. It also makes sense that, traveling through what everybody knew to be the lands of the Venetian Republic, Reverend Ólafur could mistake Milan for Venice, as we believe he did. There is no indication that Reverend Ólafur understood Italian, so he would have been at a serious disadvantage when it came to grasping the geography of the country through which he traveled.

6. The term "High Germany" (Hochdeutschland) that Reverend Ólafur uses is not much employed as a geographical designation today, but was common in his time. It referred to the southern, mountainous part of modern Austria/Germany. It is difficult to determine exactly how far into High Germany the two travelers managed to go.

God's sake to go back because all travelers on the road ahead were being killed by the soldiers of the Kaiser.[7] When he heard this, my travelling companion was very shocked.

We returned that same night down the road we had traveled, and walked for two days and two nights until we had returned to Livorno.[8] I think that it was the 22nd of October. In that town, we went to some monks and asked them for help, but they said that Luther should help us.[9] There, I had to leave my travelling companion, that good man of Hamburg. He was forced to become a sailor, since he had no money.

See, Lord, you are righteous, and your word is righteous. [c.f. Psalm 119:137.]

7. The Thirty Years' War (1618–48) had been raging for a nearly a decade, devastating the area that Reverend Ólafur and his companion were about to enter. One presumes Kaiser refers to Ferdinand II, Habsburg monarch and Holy Roman Emperor from 1619 to 1637.

8. The distance from Livorno to Monte Baldo and the Passo del Brennero is somewhere between 200 and 250 miles (320 to 400 kilometers), depending on the route. There are two obvious routes: one eastward through Florence and then north, one northwards through Parma. It seems unlikely that Reverend Ólafur would have passed by Florence and not mentioned it, so he likely went via Parma. The most direct route to Monte Baldo from Parma, however, does not go particularly near Milan (or Venice). Besides, even in good conditions with an easy road, it is hard to imagine the two men walking more than 200 miles (320 kilometers) in "four days" to get to Monte Baldo and then turning around and immediately walking the same distance in "two days and two nights" to get back. All in all, Reverend Ólafur's description of his journey is quite difficult to sort out. The fact that the various manuscript versions of *The Travels* contain different details merely compounds the problem.

9. These would have been Catholic monks. Apparently, they had scant charity for destitute Protestants.

## CHAPTER XVI About that place [Livorno], its churches, the habits of the monks, their dress, and their way of performing divine service ❧

THE TOWN OF LIVORNO is not very big, and one can walk around it in two hours. But I think it is impregnably defended. It has two very strong brick walls and a deep moat by the outside wall upon which ships may sail or row around the town. The buildings in the town are three stories high and very well built, and in many places the houses are masterfully painted.

In that town are twenty-three churches, two of them very huge, built of grey marble and decorated with gold and silver around the whole of the ceiling and the walls down to the floor. Also, the pulpit, the altar, and the seat where the monk is sitting when he takes confession are decorated thus.

While I was there, I witnessed the act of confession. The one who is going to confess takes a chair, which is separated from the monk's seat by a wide, square brass screen which stands between them. They talk to each other through this

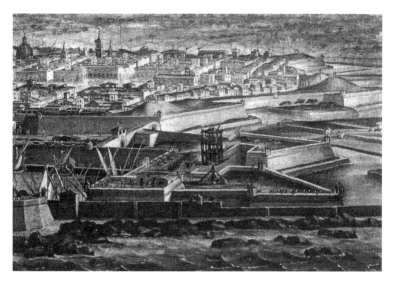

View of Livorno

screen, which is two ells in each direction and is pricked with many small holes like a sieve. If the one who is confessing gives the monk some money, then the monk releases him from sins which he is going to commit.

Alongside of each door of the church stand two pillars of black marble not more than two ells high, and upon these stand two basins with consecrated water (they say). Each person who walks into the church must dip two fingers into these basins and then make the sign of the cross on his forehead with the water, which still wets the fingers. Two old monks are set the task of observing that this is done.

Also, I saw in the town a visit made to sick people. It happened in the way I want to describe—not because there is anything to learn from it, but, because of the apish manners of they who participated, it is humorous. I witnessed this visit from the

door of the house of a Norwegian man whose name was Ólafur Símonsson, who told me what it meant.[1]

As far as I know, it happened this way. Many people, women
and men, walk along, and each holds a candle. In the middle
of this crowd walks the monk under a canopy of blue silk supported on four poles. When this procession enters the house
of a sick person, the monk is given space to walk in. The whole
crowd throws the light from their candles after him, and then
each walks back to his house.[2] The monk has a bag hung around
his neck and a small "chorus bell" which rings. In that town, the
bells never rest.

If you, good man, want to know the truth about how the
monks look, then I must tell you that they wear three different colors of clothes, depending on their religious order: some
are grey friars, some are black friars, and some are white friars. Their clothes are such that the grey friars wear long robes
which reach to their ankles. These robes are made grey because
the yarn of the warp is white, but that of the woof is black. They
do not wear anything except a shirt—no trousers. About their
necks, they have a very short mantle which is like a long hood,
so voluminous that their heads can rattle around in there.

Some of the monks wear wooden shoes, and they hold
their robes together by a wooden clasp and cord. Around them
they have a belt made of thin rope with many knots, one end

1. Ólafur Símonsson is likely the same Norwegian mentioned by Reverend
Ólafur in the preceding chapter: "the English … arranged for me a room in a house
belonging to a Norwegian man who lived in the town." Reverend Ólafur spoke
Danish (since Iceland was a Danish possession in the seventeenth century, most
Icelanders did, and certainly the educated ones), so he would have been able to
understand Norwegian sufficiently well to converse easily with his Norwegian
host.

2. It is not entirely clear what the phrase "throws the light from their candles
after him" actually means. The original Icelandic text is confused, and this is the
best sense we could make of it.

of which falls to the hem of their robes. On this rope belt they fasten their book, which has a cover, as the law books did in olden times here in Iceland. The book is at their left side, but their rosary beads are on the right. In front, they have a long tobacco pipe. They all look this way, grey, black, and white. They have their beards cut every fourteen days and their hair shaved except in a ring around their heads.

Even though they wash themselves with lye and strong soap, it would only serve to reveal their faithlessness and dishonesty all the more clearly.

How do you then dare to say: I am not impure? [c.f. Jeremiah 2:22, 23.]

CHAPTER XVII **About their dress in that town [Livorno] and the unusual things that I saw there** ᴄᴙ

THE MEN OF LIVORNO are extremely well dressed—better, I think, than anywhere else in the world, or here in the Nordic countries. They wear silk and velvet, and they wear nothing except only shirts and jerkins which are cut in five strings on the shoulders, and also the same way on the arms. Their trousers are also the same. They spend so much on themselves that their legging strings [garters] cost sixty dalers, their shoe laces ten dalers, and other things are similarly expensive. And the men who fancify themselves like this include even soldiers and porters.

In that town, food is so very expensive that people who want to buy food for the week have to pay four dalers, even for poor meals. One pound of birds (very small birds) costs sixteen shillings.[1]

1. Reverend Ólafur has Danish *skillinger* in mind here rather than English shillings. See Currencies in the Icelandic Background section of the Appendixes for a discussion of seventeenth century currencies.

About their dress on holy days, I cannot say much.

As for how the women dress: their clothing is costly and made of valuable cloth, and cut very well and very well made. The style resembles that of the lower part of honest women's dresses here in Iceland. Their bodices have gold and silver buttons, and even buttons of precious stones, and their shoes cost sixty dalers, and some more. The vamps of their shoes are made from velvet, and are divided in three on the instep with gold buttons.

All the people in that town are dark haired but white skinned, with good-looking faces and figures.

I want to put down here something that I saw, which I had never seen before. Every morning that I was there, I saw in all the streets of the town one hundred people or more going about in chains, shackled two by two together, as horses are harnessed. These people were totally naked except for a small piece of clothing around the waist to cover their "shame." Two other men went with them, whom I understood to be their overseers. With that group was a deer, from whom the antlers were cut, and also two big rams, and a fox and a sea cat [a kind of monkey], both of whom were in red dress. These two walked only on their hind legs, and wore black shoes and hats on their heads, and had blades at their sides, and—if I may say so— from behind their red trousers hung their long tails. What this act was for, I hardly know.[2]

I also saw there two other animals, which they call *buffler* [buffalo?]. These resemble the biggest ox in general shape, and they look amazingly fat. They have screwed horns like old rams.

2. We hardly know, either. The crowd of shackled, almost naked people might possibly have been a parade of slaves redeemed from North Africa. Such theatrical displays of redeemed captives, offering dramatic proof that the various Redemptionist orders had succeeded in their ransom work, were not uncommon at this time. The role of the animals Reverend Ólafur describes, however, is perplexing.

Statue of the four Barbary corsairs as captives

The Norwegian man told me that they had no fat on them, in-side or out, but that they are very strong to drag wagons filled with brick, iron, salt, and lead.[3]

Further, I saw in that town a masterpiece, the like of which I have never seen before or since. It was four human figures, in fetters, cast in copper [i.e., bronze], about a column of white marble. This column was foursquare, and a figure sat by each side, looking almost like living men. These were replicas of a Turk and his three sons, who had done great damage to Chris-tianity. In stature, they were like giants, but the duke of that town had conquered them in battle and had had their figures cast in memory of his victory. His figure stands over them with

3. This "Norwegian man" is, presumably, Ólafur Símonsson, the Norwegian mentioned in previous chapters.

a big sword in hand.[4] There, on pikes on a wall, are placed the severed heads of Turkish pirates.[5]

Scripture says that bad fortune will overcome the godless. [c.f. Job 8:13.]

4. This statue, known in Italian as *Il Monumento dei Quattro Mori* (the Monument of the Four Moors), contains two sections. The upper part was created by Giovanni Bandini and erected in 1617. It depicts Ferdinando I (Ferdinando de' Medici (1549–1609), the grand duke of Tuscany). The four "Turks" in the lower part were created by Pietro Tacca, in 1623–26. Reverend Ólafur is quite likely the first person to mention the *Quattro Mori* in a book. The statue can still be seen in Livorno today.

5. When Reverend Ólafur visited it, Livorno was a thriving and prosperous port with a population of around ten thousand. Its prosperity derived from more than simple trade, though. The city had its own corsairs (the Order of the Knights of Saint Stephen, created in the 1560s) who attacked Muslim vessels in the Mediterranean, returning with booty and captives to be enslaved or ransomed. At the same time, merchants who bought merchandise seized from captured European ships in Tripoli, Tunis, and Algiers could resell it profitably in the Livorno markets. (It is no coincidence that Reverend Ólafur was put aboard a Livorno-bound ship when he left Algiers.) Despite its realpolitik trading relations with North Africa, the city had a reputation for being implacably hostile toward Barbary corsairs: hence the pikes on the wall.

CHAPTER XVIII **About my travels to Genoa and from there to Marseilles** ℭℜ

FROM LIVORNO IN ITALY, I bought passage on a small boat—which they call a barque—to that great and powerful town Genoa by the border of the French kingdom. I was two days on that voyage. Genoa is an enormously great city, with very strongly built walls. It is by the sea, with huge castles on both sides, and with cannons so large that one could almost crawl into their mouths. I was told that the city is eighteen great miles around.[1] Where it meets the sea, it is twelve stories high and triple-walled.[2] Genoa stands under the mountains which are named Alpesfjöll [the Alps].

1. It is hard to know for certain, but by "great mile," Reverend Ólafur likely intends some version of the German *große Meile*, which equaled approximately 5–6 statute miles (8–9.5 kilometers). Once again, though, his estimate of the size of a city seems inflated, since his measurement would mean the circumference of Genoa was something like 90 miles (145 kilometers) (18 x 5 = 90). *Cook's Handbook to Northern Italy* (1881) states that Genoa's "inner walls comprise a circuit of seven miles, and the broad rampart of the outer walls is no less than twenty miles in circumference." Even if we assume the circuit of the seventeenth century city's walls to have been the same as that of the nineteenth century city's, this is still a long way from 90 miles.
2. Genoa, like Milan and many other Italian cities, had protective walls. As

58

In that place, a Danish woman accommodated me for two nights and helped me in other things.

From each place one travels, then he must buy a "letter" to another, which is testimony that he is not a sick or infected person. For that letter of testimony, one has to pay four *stifur* [copper coins]—which is as much as three fish here in Iceland for us.[3]

On the way [to Genoa] I saw the glow of Rome in the distance. Although I did not see the city itself, during the night I saw the hills of the city and the glowing lights of it, which seemed to mount higher in the sky than the constellation of Pisces—which is seen in mid-sky there. From that route only four stars are to be seen. This, they told me, was Rome.[4]

I came to Genoa on the 28th of October. There were not many things of interest there that I had not already seen earlier, except for three reindeer, and a tamed bear which did not walk except on its hind legs, and kept its front legs behind its back. There I first saw a stained-glass window, at least five or six fathoms high. And there, too, I saw for the first time windmills, at which I stared. I also saw a brick house which was unusually constructed. It was glossy on the outside, and in it wine was

---

the city expanded over the centuries, the walls were improved and enlarged. The first extensive set of walls was built in the ninth century. A second, larger set was added in the twelfth century. These were expanded in the fourteenth century and then enlarged and fortified in the sixteenth century. A new spate of wall construction was just under way when Reverend Ólafur visited the city, the Genoese Doge of the time (Giacomo Lomellini) having officiated at a ceremony in December 1626 in which he laid the first stone of the new walls. Reverend Ólafur's description of the city as being "triple-walled" is not literally accurate, at least not in the sense of there being three clearly demarcated, concentric walls. "Multi-walled" might be a more appropriate description.

3. In Iceland at this period, fish was treated as a unit of currency in business and trade.

4. Clearly, Reverend Ólafur was mistaken, or misled (as he seemingly suspects himself). It is a geographical impossibility to see the lights of Rome along the route he was sailing.

kept. This house seemed to me to be four fathoms large on each side. I did not know how it was equipped inside, but there was an iron ladder outside which was fastened to a brick column.

From Genoa, I bought again passage on a ship—on All Saints Day morning [November 1]—to Marseilles, in France, with help from the Danish woman. On the 6th day of that month, I came to the town called Blikmar [?], in France. Every night during that voyage, we went close ashore; the captain and crew of the ship did not dare anything else because of the [Barbary] pirates. On the 7th day of that month, I came to Marseilles and gave the master of the town my passport from the Turkish pirates. That day, I did not get any place to stay in the town till evening—though I tearfully begged in over twenty places. At sunset, a woman came to me where I sat mournfully. She talked to me in correct Icelandic and asked, "What manner of man are you?" I answered her: "A poor miserable Icelander." "Are you an Icelander?" she said. "Then come with me. I will give you a room tonight. I am also an Icelander, a woman also exiled."

But when I came to her house, there were both a German man and some English there who understood my words. One of the English men, who was a spectacle maker, recognized me. This man said that I was a priest from Iceland. Then the woman immediately ordered me out of the house. When she seized me and tried to throw me out, my good God "awaked" the German merchant. He became concerned at once and got straight up from the drinking table—because it was a drinking house—and he promised to pay for my food and drink and to house me as long as I was in that town.

In the bitterness and adversity of life, we are guided by God to relief.

## CHAPTER XIX About what happened to me in Marseilles and what prevented me from traveling to Paris ❧

THAT EVENING I got enough to eat and drink, and also a good bed to rest in, none of which had I got since I had first been captured sixteen weeks and one day before. Aboard ship, I had had to lie down on ropes, and I had not even had a proper chance to take my clothes off, neither night nor day. When I came to this house, I had only four pieces of bread in a small sack of cloth (I had brought eighteen from Italy) and had four dalers left of my money, which I kept well.

The next morning, very early, the merchant whom I have already mentioned came and confirmed the promise he had made to aid me. He declared before everybody that, although he did not know what caused him to feel so, he loved me as his own father. I stayed in that house, at his expense, during the 8th, 9th, and until early on the 10th day of that month, which was a Saturday.

On that day, five Dutch sea captains came into the drinking house, sat down, and began drinking good wine. Around that time food was brought to me where I sat at a small table. While I was eating, the most important of the captains asked me who I was, where I came from, and where I was going. When I had told him my story, he was so moved that he stood up from his table, walked over to me where I sat in my poverty, took me in his arms, and promised to give me food and drink on his ship as long as he made his trade. He also promised that he would bring me with him to Holland and also that he would see me to Denmark.[1] This honest fellow's name was Caritas Hardspenner. When he walked out of that house, he called me to come with him, and I went with him straight to his ship. I was there with him for six weeks and two days while his ship was in the harbor and went with him almost daily into the town.

At that time, I wanted to travel to Paris, that capital of the kingdom of France, which is the royal residence, twelve miles from Marseilles, straight north.[2] Several things, however, prevented me from doing this: 1) I was very weak and did not trust myself able to make the walk; 2) I was very poor, and it always costs something to travel in those countries; 3) I had no proper clothes to wear, and I was ashamed to be amongst people because of the wretchedness of my plight, my appearance, and the sorrow which I had (and still have today); 4) I had heard

1. It is unclear what language the captain and Reverend Ólafur might have conversed in. There is little chance that Reverend Ólafur spoke Dutch. Perhaps they used German. We are not likely to ever know.

2. Reverend Ólafur seems to have no clear grasp of the geography involved here. The overland distance between Marseilles and Paris is about 500 statute miles (800 kilometers). Whether he intends here the same "mile" he employed when assessing the circumference of Milan/Venice (one such "mile" equaled 7.5 statute miles), or "great miles" (one "great mile" equaled 5–6 statute miles [8–9.5 kilometers]), or some other version of a "mile" entirely, he is still way off.

Dutch sea captain with
navigational instruments

rumors of murder being committed on the road, and was too
faint-hearted because of my misery to chance the trip.

When I am poor, I am rich, for I fear God and avoid sin.
Proverbs 12; Tob. 4; Luke 7.[3]

3. Tobias (Tob.) is one of the books of the Apocrypha, or Deutero-canonical
books.

CHAPTER XX  About some of the
handwork and practices which I
saw there for providing food for
the people ☙

IN THAT TOWN [Marseilles], I did not see many things that
I had not seen in the other places (and have already written
about) except for some handwork and some methods of providing food from the sea.

There I saw two great ships being built. First, the keel is
laid. Next, the ribs are placed in the shape which the ship will
take. Then the ribs are lined. Then, lastly, the planks forming
the hull are put on.

I also paid a visit to a smithy where big anchors are made.
In this place, the wind hammers the iron; the sledgehammers
come from the air and some come from a conical wheel, above
which stand two mills. Of that apparatus, I did not have any
understanding at all.[1] The anchors are moved into the furnace

1. Reverend Ólafur seems to be describing a kind of windmill-powered trip-
hammer, a device to mechanically drive the sledgehammers that beat the hot
iron—a technology entirely beyond anything he had ever seen before.

by wheels. In another smithy, I saw iron cutters large and small. I also visited the place where copper [bronze] cannon are cast. The building of that smithy stood quite tall. I think that their molds were located under the forge's heart. But about that I cannot talk with any true knowledge.

Now, about their manner of food supply.

First, the fishermen go out day after day with extremely long nets, but get little profit of it in my opinion. Some get a few small trout, no bigger than minnows. Some get nothing except what we here in Iceland call *ígulker* [sea urchins], and only one small basket of such. And this is their maintenance all of their lives, for both them and their wives and children.

In that town fresh food is very expensive. There is good and plentiful drink there, consisting of French wine, which is not served except equally with water.

Also there are fishermen who, with their wives and children, live from what they catch in the rounded pool [harbor] that the town surrounds—which I will talk about later. They go out in a small boat. The wife rows while the husband stands in the bow with a long pole in his hands. At the end of that pole is a rather big dip-net woven of cord. Inside the wooden frame of the net are set five or six teeth of iron. With these teeth, he scratches down to the sea bottom, and when he has got the dip-net full of dirt, then the wife lets go the oars and helps him to draw the dip-net up to the gunwale so that he can rinse the dirt from it. After this, there remains in the dip-net one dab [a small flat fish], sometimes two or three, sometimes none.

Also there are fishing methods such that, every morning, two men go out in a boat with nets supported by four big curved brackets tied together at the end of a long pole which is raised up in the bow of the boat. There is a large stone at the lower end of the pole to hold it in place. When these fishermen come to other ships which have nets thrown out, they put their own net down, and they get a few trout, sometimes six, seven, or eight. In this way, they maintain themselves and their families.[2]

My brothers, there is poverty in more places than in Iceland.

There are many people who become panicked over nothing, and, in their blind haste, hinder their own arrival on shore. On the other hand, there are those who stay calm though they may be in great need and very weak and miserable. Upon these people, God looks with mercy and helps them in their distress—as he has done for me.

2. Compared to the fishing in Icelandic waters, the catches Reverend Ólafur witnessed would have seemed paltry indeed.

## CHAPTER XXI About Marseilles itself, the dress of the inhabitants, both men and women, and about my travels from there ☙

MARSEILLES IS BUILT about a rounded fjord which is so narrow that I think it must be less than forty fathoms wide across the fjord mouth. In the channel are four brick towers between which are strung very strong iron chains. Large iron points stick out from these chains, so that ships or boats cannot sail in or out of there in any way. On the side of the fjord mouth stands the castle of that place. Three large tree trunks are fastened there in the water, forming a long, floating boom, closed at one end but open at the other, which are locked to the castle. The harbor is located inside this log boom and can contain at least one hundred ships.

Marseilles is a large town, with many buildings that are five, and, in some places, six stories high. The whole is protected by cannons much larger than any I saw anywhere else on my miserable travels. No one can pass out or in without permission of those in the castle.

The men and women in that town wear the same fashion of clothes as in Italy. They do not lay quite as much stress on dressing, but they are very clean. The people are dark haired and white skinned.

In that town, I saw, on the Saint Andrew's Mass, a group of 1,400 women who walked their "vow walk," as is their custom, to Saint Andrew's Church, which stood to the eastward, close to the town, in a cloister—whether it was a nunnery or a monastery, I did not know.[1] This host of women was most pleasant to look upon. They all had linen aprons, white as snow, which they drew together at their belts, and which were woven in such a way as to come together on the mid back.

Their order of walking in this procession was that, first, they walked side by side, two, then three, four, five and six, seven, eight, nine, ten, and each row was wider than the one before it, but there was no row of more than ten.

Now, about my leaving there.

We went from that town on Christmas Eve, according to my reckoning, and then we waited outside for two days for our captain. Two other Dutch ships also waited for him, since he was friend to them all and he had the biggest ship and the most cannons. On the third morning, twelve ships left in one fleet together. Only three of them were armed. The ship I was on had 26 cannons and 8 *steinstykki*.[2] Another ship had 24 cannons and 6 steinstykki. The third ship had 12 smaller cannons.

1. The feast day of St. Andrew is November 30.
2. The literal meaning of steinstykki is "stone pieces," but *stykki* in this context is a loanword from the Danish for "cannon." Steinstykki refers to cannons that fired stone balls rather than iron or lead shot. In other European languages, these weapons were known variously as pattaroees, patteraroes, pedereros, pedreros, or pettereros. All these terms derive from Spanish *piedra* or Portuguese *pedra*, both meaning "stone." Pattaroees were generally small-sized, breech-loading (as

View of Marseilles

We had the best wind for nine days. On the tenth day of Christmas, during the best weather of all, we sailed through the Straits of Gibraltar, as they call it. The captains and crew had great anxiety because [Barbary] pirates normally lurk there. There is a deadly enmity between the Spanish and the Dutch, and therefore we sailed as close as possible to the Barbari Coast. After that, we did not see land until we came close to England from the north, on the 23rd of January. We then sailed calmly along for three days. One night, we almost beached on a skerry because we then had a little bad wind.

Eleven days before Pálsdagur, the 25th of January, I lost that night my vest which I had washed and hung in the ship's ropes.[3] The crew unwittingly clambered over it and knocked it off. I thus did not have anything to cover me except an old shirt and the breeches in which I had been captured. Soon thereafter, I lost my hat off my head because of the weather. Then my honest friend Captain Caritas gave me another hat, which was small, and a steersman gave me an old pullover, and I bought another myself.

Wherever men travel, there are robbers, both on sea and land, so we must trust in God's mercy. Murder and burning are customarily done in those countries. At sea, robbery and killing are common to hear of. On our voyage, we twice encountered two pirate ships, but they left us alone.

On the 8th of February, we came so close to Holland that we first saw the towers of the towns. The sea was not more than four fathoms deep, and therefore Holland will always be invincible because the sea shoals so gradually from the shore. There were more than 100 stranded ships there, stuck immov-

---

opposed to muzzle-loading) swivel guns. They were fairly common in Reverend Ólafur's time.

3. Pálsdagur is "Paul's Day," a religious holiday in Iceland.

Seventeenth century Dutch "round-bottomed" sailing ships

ably. They must unload cargo from the ships more than three sea miles from the shore. For every 60 tons of cargo carried to land, they [the local authorities] are given 30 dalers [as duty]. It took two days to unload the ship, and then we removed to Enkeysen, and I came to Holland.[4]

Ah, you, good God's man, I can tell you of God's promise which he gives to those whom he has mercy upon: do not be afraid, I have saved you and called you by name; you are mine, and when you cross the waters I will be with you, so that the flood will not drown you. [Isaiah 41:1.]

4. "Enkeysen" is Reverend Ólafur's rendering of Enkhuizen. Enkhuizen is located on what is now the IJsselmeer, a large, shallow (16–20 feet/5–6 meters), artificial freshwater lake reclaimed from the sea in the 1930s. In Reverend Ólafur's day, this body of water would have been the Zuiderzee, saltwater instead of fresh, but just as shallow. His observation that "the sea was not more than four fathoms deep" is reassuringly accurate, since 4 fathoms equals 24 feet. In the 1620s, Enkhuizen had a population of about 21,000 and in importance as a port was second only to Amsterdam.

### CHAPTER XXII  About what happened to me in Holland, and about that country and its places ↶

WHEN I CAME INTO the town on that big ship on which I had been traveling,[1] my good Captain Caritas came back on-board and gave me further permission to have food on it, as long as I should be there. He said he would look after things so that I could easily come to Denmark. Then he added to that help he had already given me so far (both in France and on the way) by giving me two good shirts, although they were old, and also leggings and shoes. Before Christmas, in France, he had given me one of his frockcoats, which cost twelve guilders—equaling five dalers in their reckoning.[2] This coat was all I had had for cover-ing, night and day, along with a large hat like a monk's hat.

When I had been four days in the town on this big ship, I became short of food for myself and a cabin boy, who had been kept aboard the ship because he had stolen food and sold it for

1. The town was Enkhiuzen.
2. The "daler" Reverend Ólafur refers to here is, again, the Danish rigsdaler. The exchange rate he gives is in line with other sources for this period.

4. Mid-seventeenth century Holland

money for himself. Then I had to leave the ship and planned to search for Captain Caritas's house, but I did not have success in this because the town was so big. I came upon one house where there was a Danish man and a Norwegian woman, and there I got a room for myself. I think that it was the 23rd of February. I was there in that house till the 16th of March, on very poor provisions because my purse was so light. During that time, I traveled to Hornstaður[3] because I owed there to a sailor of one of the ships nine stuiver, that is 18 shillings [skillings]. Then I returned to Enkeysen [Enkhuizen].

Now about the countryside and the towns. The Dutch countryside is such that, wherever I went, as far as I could tell, it was manmade. All around the land are pole fences sunk down to the seabed, made of a tree whose wood becomes like stone in

3. "Hornstaður" is Reverend Ólafur's rendering of Hoorn, a port town located about 12 miles (20 kilometers) west-by-southwest of Enkhuizen.

the sea. Then stones, bought from other countries, are placed against the fences. Clay, which looks like peat here in Iceland, is then shoveled over the rocks. Seen from a distance, the land is lower than the sea outside.

There are windmills throughout the whole country that draw up from the land the water which seeps in from the sea. These windmills work night and day when the wind blows. There are so many that in between them there is no more distance than a racecourse. Here, it is said that if the wind would not blow for a month, then the country would be under water.

Many of the buildings in the towns which I saw there were very well built. Normally, they are no more than three, or at most four, stories high. Some of them are painted outside and in with all kinds of different colors, and many of them are decorated with great skill.

Ships lay at anchor [on canals] amongst the houses and not outside, except when cargo is loaded or unloaded. Where the Dutch first see a sandy spit or shallow shoal, they shovel out a big outlet and throw the clay from the sea bottom up on both sides. After a year, the clay is hard as stone. The towns which I visited were built on such ridges of clay. Across the canals that are thus formed in these towns are surprisingly huge bridges made with great skill. Some of these can be drawn up and down in order to let ships pass. On both sorts, horses are ridden and carriages driven. To maintain these canals, ten men from the town are normally retained, who go along these canals in shallow boats with poles in their hands. They wear boots which come up to their armpits. At the lower end of their poles they have what look like wool cards with five or six wide teeth made of iron. They dredge the canals and place the mud or clay that comes out wherever the town's authorities tell them. After a year, it is hard as stone, and then new houses are built. And so the towns expand year after year, with the dates being marked on each house door.

## CHAPTER XXIII About my travels to Fleyland [the island of Vlieland, Holland] and to Krónuborg [Kronborg, on the island of Zealand, Denmark] and my reception there ℘

ON THE 16TH OF MARCH, I got passage on a ship with another Dutch captain through the intercession of my good friend and helper Captain Caritas, whom I have mentioned before.

As for the people of Holland, in all respects, both in appearance and conduct, they are unlike any other. They are humane and benevolent, particularly the sailors. Nowhere else are the women as good looking, for the Dutch women can be said to be very beautiful. The religion of these people, I think, is mixed.

The captain with whom I went from Holland was named Ulf Racheit, and I spent 23 days with him on his ship. I was also with him in Fleyland for two days,[1] in that town which

1. By "Fleyland," Reverend Ólafur seems to be referring to what today is known as Vlieland, which is one of the West Frisian Islands, a chain of islands

Kronborg, the Danish coastal fortress

is called Rolbýr.[2] In that land, I saw no grassy plants, nothing except red sand.

Sixty-five ships sailed together from Fleyland, most of them headed to Denmark to buy oxen, which during the springtime do not cost much. We sailed from Fleyland on the 22nd and had very fair wind and came towards Jótlandsskagi [the Jutland Peninsula] on the 25th. On the 26th, we sighted the Swedish kingdom.

I came to Krónuborg in Denmark and felt almost as if I had arrived home in Iceland.[3] Directly when I came to the town,

---

running parallel to the Dutch coast. Vlieland is situated just north of what was then the Zuiderzee and is now the artificial freshwater lake of IJsselmeer.

2. It is difficult to know exactly which town Reverend Ólafur is referring to here.

3. "Krónuborg" is Reverend Ólafur's rendering of Kronborg, which is located in present-day Helsingør on the northeastern tip of Zealand Island, on the sound between Zealand and Sweden. Kronborg was built in the early fifteenth

I met there an honest man, Jakob Pétursson, who had earlier been a sheriff for seven years in the Westman Islands. He took me at once into his house, where his wife and children were. After a meal, he was called to attend the funeral of a merchant, and see him to his grave. I went with him there and heard the funeral sermon. Later that night, I was invited with him as a guest of the priest who had preached the funeral sermon. That man asked me many things, but his name I have forgotten. That night, this same priest invited several men to a gathering—which I and Jakob thought he did because he hoped they would have pity on me. But it did not help. He himself, however, gave me a daler and a good old hat. Although they had many children, Jakob and his wife gave me an old shirt, a worn priest's collar, and a new, small *postilla* [book of sermons].

Now it is written by the prophet that Nebuzaradan gave him conscience money and sent him away. [Jeremiah 39:13.]

---

century to control access to the Baltic Sea—the sound is only about 2.5 miles (4 kilometers) wide at that point. By Reverend Ólafur's day, the original medieval fortress had been extensively renovated. Helsingør is the inspiration for "Elsinore" in Shakespeare's *Hamlet*, and Kronborg, for the castle.

CHAPTER XXIV About my arrival in
Copenhagen, my good reception,
and donations from honest men,
learned and not ꙮ

ON THE 28TH OF MARCH, I came to Copenhagen, and
as soon as I got there, I was received as if I were an angel. The
man who was closest to me and most concerned about my well-
being was an honorable man named Jens Hesselberg, who had
been king's man on the Westman Islands for some time.[1] That
same day, he brought me to the Compagniet and told the honest Icelandic shipowners about me.[2] They took me into their
hands, and, at his request, gave me free board for seven and a
half weeks, also clothing for Easter, which they themselves had
made for me and paid for—either themselves or my honest Jens.

On the first day I came there, I was given several small coins
(exactly two dalers) by some [of the Dutch?] sailors who knew

1. A "king's man" was a combination sheriff and tax collector.
2. "Compagniet" is short for Det Islandske, Færöiske og Nordlandske Kom-
pagni, the Trading Company of Iceland, the Faeroe Islands, and the Northland
(established in 1620).

View of Copenhagen from the sea (c. 1640)

me. Thanks and glory be to God, always! On the 5th of April, I, poor man, was invited, along with Master Þorlákur Skúlason, to a company of guests at Doctor Hans Resen's house.[3] Here I was asked many things by him about all the countries which I had been to, including Iceland. He gave me a daler.

On the 8th of April, I got an opportunity to see his most gracious majesty, the noble-born King Kristján [Christian] of

3. "Doctor Hans Resen" must have been Hans Poulson Resen, who was the Sjálandsbiskup (the bishop of Sjælland, i.e., Zealand, the island on which Copenhagen is located), the leader of the Danish, and so also of the Icelandic, Church.

Denmark and Norway, the fourth of that name with the royal title. This gracious Lord seems to be humble and gentle with his subjects. That same day, I saw his noble-born son, the prince, the honorable Kristján the Fifth.

During this month I was invited to many gatherings, along with many guests, by honorable men, and I often enjoyed the goodness of many kind men, especially the Icelandic merchants, and so I acquired in that most respectable place nearly eighteen dalers. But because of my distress and poorness, I had to spend them all.

To show my gratitude before God and all good men, I want to name those who helped me in that honorable town. The first one who gave to me was a merchant who sails to the Faeroe Islands, with support of my honest Jens Heselberg. The next was an Icelander named Bjarni Ormsson, who had once held authority in the Westman Islands; he gave me two dalers and helped me in other things. The next was an honorable woman who had also held authority in the Westman Islands; she gave me two dalers as well, and offered me food and drink free during my stay in the town. Mats Hansson, an honest merchant from North Iceland, then in Copenhagen, gave me six dalers of that money which the honorable priests from North Iceland, the Reverends Þorsteinn Illugason and Bjarni Gamlason, had given as pension to Icelandic priests in Denmark, for which the Lord himself will reward them. Also, one of those honorable priests, whose name was Mister Marteinn, gave me two dalers. A schoolmaster gave me two dalers, and an Icelander who had been brought up on the Westman Islands also gave me a daler.

I think this will prove the truth of what I have said: in that royal town, many good things are done.

In Copenhagen, there are many fine and masterly preachers—God be thanked. And there is very fine order in all things.

Also, nowhere is there better beer drunk or better food cooked, and nowhere as comfortable a bed as there, wherever I came to.

About the town and the buildings in it, I do not need to write because many good men have been there and know it very well.

The town, though, was in a sad and sorrowful condition because of the war.[4] May it please God, because of His love of mankind, to stop the fighting and to show grace and mercy upon our king and all his noble-born house to strengthen and support him.

All victories come from God, as can be read in the Bible: Genesis: 4; Exodus: 17; Deuteronomy: 2; John: 11.

4. The Thirty Years' War.

CHAPTER XXV **About my complaint, which I had to relate to everyone, and about how I was incapacitated by my sorrows, and about what sorrow and pain may do for us** ଓଃ

MY DEAR, BELOVED READER and good friend, I must confess that, because of the loss of my wife and children, which God himself heals, I cannot talk or write as I want or should about our merciful lord the king, the prince, the son of the king, the town of Copenhagen, the lords there, the preachers there, or whatever else I saw and heard there. During the time that I spent in Denmark and got to know how sorrowfully the events of the war had gone and the great loss of property which the Crown had suffered, my sorrow became too great, because then all my hope was lost—which was that I would get some support [ransom money] there, so that I could buy free my wife and children.[1] I was always optimistic, for it could well have

1. Under King Christian IV, Denmark had entered the Thirty Years' War in 1624. In August 1626, a little over a year and a half before Reverend Ólafur's visit

happened if everything had gone well for our king. And that proverb has been proved true for me, which is widely common among people, that "seldom is a great grief alone."

But the will of God decides everything. My choice in these matters, in these mournful days of distress, is none else than to flee to the Lord and to still hope for His mercy, both for me and my family, and all others who have walked or will walk the path of distress and adversity. The Holy Spirit may be called the Eternal Father, for I believe that He will not remove His fatherly heart from His children, although He still punishes them, because the cross is the load which He lets his children bear, for the well-being of themselves and others, because the people who are God's children are surely resigned to that cross—which not only can be seen from the texts clearly, but it can obviously be seen from the patriarchs, the prophets, the apostles, the martyrs, and all the saints and examples of holiness.

About this, King David says: "The righteous may suffer much, but the Lord saves them from all" [Psalm 34:19]. And Christ himself says: "He who wants to follow me must deny himself and take this cross on himself every day and walk my road" [Luke 9:23]. The scribes and painters who depict the nature of the animals write that when the swan is sick and has come close to death, his songs are of the greatest beauty. But my nature is not that way, unfortunately. I let myself get distressed, although God treats me as He is wont to do with His children—which is for my own and others' good. Firstly, God lays the cross of suffering upon us so that His blessed name should be praised, for when, against human reason, He helps us again, as He has done for me, people see clearly how to know

---

to Copenhagen, the Danes suffered a major defeat at Lutter am Barenberge, just south of what is now Hanover, Germany. As a result, the royal coffers were seriously depleted, and the king gave Reverend Ólafur no ransom money.

His existence, His love, faith, yes, and omnipotence. Secondly, the cross lies on the faithful so they shall not think that they are innocent. As the prophet says: "I will punish you with mercy so that you do not think that you are free of guilt." Thirdly, God lays the cross on Christians in order to test them to see if they—regardless of whether they are doing well or badly—still want to love God with all their hearts and live "under the cross."

I perceive all this, but, though I am in great weakness, my "singing voice," which I have trained and tamed in times of sorrow, remains the same—which perhaps should not be. But I imitate in this not the swan but the raven, which cries the same way when he is crushed and dying as he does when still alive. May God have pity on me, a wretched sinner. I ask almighty God for patience because it can "beat sorrow to death," since long-lasting sorrow brings no reward except that which is bad, and therefore I want to raise my head and heart and think that God is the one who both creates men and rules men and has the power and can always give consolation with joy after the burden of the cross. As King David tells me: "Wait for the Lord." Also, Saint Paul says: "In our times of temptation, we tell ourselves that suffering gives patience." [Romans 5:3.]

## CHAPTER XXVI About my voyage from Copenhagen to Iceland and how I was received when I came there ❧

I SPENT SEVEN and a half weeks in that highly respected town of Copenhagen. There, where I had a room, my food and drink cost a total of 19 dalers for two meals a day during the time I was there. On the 4th of May, I went from Copenhagen to Krónuborg and stayed there with Jakob Pétursson till the 24th. Then I boarded ship, again with the Dutch, with whom I sailed to the Westman Islands. I was at Krónuborg till the 6th of June because, at that time, the weather was constantly stormy from the north. Thereafter, we sailed with a fair wind, 42 ships in a fleet, among which were 17 ships headed for Iceland.

We were 31 days on that voyage, since we did not get even one day of fair wind. On the 13th of June, all these ships had to take shelter in a small bay called Flekurey, and there we spent five days.[1] There, I visited a few farm steadings, and I very much

1. It is not altogether clear why the convoy had to spend five days at Flekurey (southwest of Kristiansand, on the Norwegian coast). Bad weather is the reason

liked my stay there. On the 17th day of that month, we went from there with a mild wind from the east. We were driven off course towards Scotland, and so to the Orkneys on the 27th. We came in sight of Iceland on the 4th of July, and on the 6th to the Westman Islands. When I came there, the poor people received me as if I had been their own best friend returned again from death. Some of those honest men and women proved themselves to be kindly and generous. My poor daughter and that honest Oddur Pétursson took me in and cared for me.[2] The 7th day of that month, I went onto the mainland and met there my beloved fellow neighbors, relatives, and good friends, who received me with complete joy and did everything for me that they could— so much that I cannot write it all. On the 9th day of that month, I was able to meet with that most honest Bishop Oddur Einarsson and his honorable wife, who joyfully took me in as if I had been their own true son whom they had got back from death.[3] I left there with kind gifts of money and good support.

God should always be praised by all people, but good men should also be thanked by a man in great need. The Reverend Gísli Oddsson and his honourable wife, the Reverends Snæbjörn Stefánsson, Jón Sigurðsson, and Jón Bergsson, also Erlendur Ásmundsson, Þorleifur Magnússon, and, later, the king's

---

implied in the text, but it might have been that the ships had to stop there to pass through customs.

2. This is the same Oddur Pétursson, mentioned in Kláus Eyjólfsson's report, who stood upon the Háin (the mountain that overlooked the harbor on Heimaey) and watched the events of the corsair raid unfold. He was a captain on one of the fishing boats operating out of Heimaey. In 1636 his boat sank and he drowned. That same fishing season three fishing boats sank in the waters around Heimaey: altogether, 45 men drowned. Among them was Eyjólfur Sölmundsson, the husband of Guðríður Símonardóttir (whose letter to him from Algiers appears in the Letters section).

3. Oddur Einarsson was one of the two bishops of Iceland at the time. His seat was at Skálholt, in South Iceland.

man Gísli Hákonarson and his honorable wife, Margrét, from Bræðratunga, and my in-laws and relations—all these people were very kind and generous to me.

God opens the hearts of men and showers mercy upon those who most need it. All good gifts come from our Father in Heaven above. [James 1:17.]

## CHAPTER XXVII  About the comfort and consolation that we get from the words of God; He tells us to pray for help and promises us a hearing, and of this we have examples ❦

HOW AND FOR WHAT and to whom we should pray, and to whom we should call out, is given us in scripture (Matthew: 6; Luke: 18). There, the Lord Christ gives us the parable of the unrighteous judge and the imploring widow, and, afterwards, says the truth himself: "Hear what the unrighteous judge saith. Shall not God avenge his own elect, which cry day and night unto him, though he bear long with them? I tell you that He will avenge them speedily." How, then, can a brokenhearted, sorrowful man not feel joy that the Lord is so merciful to all who need help? As David, too, says (Psalms: 134, 45). Plutarch writes this way about King Demetrius, that he let a petition of his subordinates fall into the flowing water so that he would not have to answer them.

The world is a merciless, cruel place to its children when they are most in need, but heavenly charity is always available to those who pray to the Lord in the name of Jesus. I can affirm, with examples, that God certainly wants to answer our prayers when we pray as He wants us to. We have enough pledges and promises—praised shall be God!—both in the Old and New Testament. "Implore me and pray in your distress. I am with you in your distress and want to free you from it." Christ himself confirms this with a simple oath that God wants to hear the prayers of those who call upon Him. Verily, I tell you that, when we pray, whether it is for ourselves or for others, we should remember that God has, in His own words, promised to hear our prayers; therefore, He can do nothing else than as He has promised. All men are liars, and their words may fail sometimes, but the Lord's words are true: He keeps His promise.

Look at the old examples and mark them well. In them, nobody is chided who has prayed to God. (Syr. 3.) Moses' prayer was so strong that it not only parted the Red Sea and overcame the Amalekites but "overcame" God himself, so that He did not destroy the hard-tempered people of Israel in His anger. The prayers of the three men in the furnace took the power from the fire. Yes, God has a most generous hand, much more generous than we have the tongue, the mouth, or the heart to know how to desire. Abraham desired nothing of God but that Ishmael could live, but received in answer from God that his wife should give birth to a young son, with whom the Lord wanted to establish a covenant with his seed after him. Therefore, should Ishmael not only live after his conception but also be blessed and grow and reproduce. Solomon desired wisdom from God, and God not only fulfilled his wish, but, rather, gave him so much of wisdom and judicious heart that his equal never existed, either before or since. Yes, God gave him that which he did not pray for, which was wealth and honor, and he had no equal among kings. That prodigal son got more than what he desired.

Upon this and similar examples, and God's promises, we should, with courage, walk towards the "chair of mercy" so that we may receive mercy both for ourselves and for others, after God's word.

# Afterword ❧

THE TEXT OF *The Travels* finishes at this point, but we know the end of the story from other sources. After his return, Reverend Ólafur continued to live on Heimaey. In 1636, thirty-five of the enslaved Icelanders were finally ransomed. Twenty-seven of these eventually returned safely to Iceland. Among this group was Reverend Ólafur's wife. The two of them had nearly three full years together before he died, at the age of 75, on March 1, 1639.

Reverend Ólafur and his wife never saw any of their abducted children again.

# Letters,
# Appendixes,
# Suggestions for
# Further Reading
# & Index

# Letters ℭ℞

A NUMBER OF LETTERS concerning the Tyrkjaránið (the "Turkish" corsair raid of July, 1627) have survived. Most were written by captives and sent from the Barbari to family and friends back in Iceland. One letter is a chronicle of the raid pieced together from the eyewitness accounts of people who managed to evade capture. We have placed this one first in the series.

Not only do these letters provide a valuable source of added detail, both about the Tyrkjaránið itself and about conditions in the Barbari, they also give modern readers a compelling first-hand glimpse into the human cost of the event.

# Kláus Eyjólfsson

The chronicle of Kláus Eyjólfsson, member of the Lögrétta [the legislature of the Icelandic parliament], concerning the incursions that the Turks made on the Westman Islands from the 17th to the 19th of July 1627.

OF THE ORIGINS of the Turkish expedition, I cannot myself accurately or truthfully write. But some of those who escaped captivity maintain that two lords of the Turkish empire made a bet with each other, one wagering against the other that it would not be possible to get even the smallest stone out of Iceland, much less a man. Because of this wager, the expedition was prepared and equipped, and twelve ships were sent to Iceland to capture as many people as possible and bring them back unharmed, for it is said that even one infant could fetch as much as three hundred dalers in Algeria.

When the fleet reached Iceland, it dispersed. Two ships arrived at the East Fjords and stopped in Djúpivogur in Berufjörður fjord. There they were seen late during the day. One cruised the harbor and quickly captured a merchant ship, putting the Danish crew in fetters and taking everything they thought to be useful. The crew of the other ship went up inland to the farmhouses with great noise and wickedness.

The first person they encountered was a young man. They took him at once and bound him and left him lying there. Then they captured other people, both men and women, driving them like sheep are driven to the pen. Those who could not walk, the wounded or the weak, the crippled or blind, they struck down and killed. And because those Turkish blood-hounds could never sate their desire for the blood of the inno-cent, they coursed like dogs or wild beasts, and so came all the way to Eydalir, what is much more than an Icelandic þingman-naleið from where they first came to shore.[1]

It is reliably reported that they captured and brought to their ship many people, both young and old together. But the young man whom they first took and bound lay there until they went again to the sea. Then they sliced open his forehead and pulled his scalp down over his eyes and slashed his buttocks.[2]

When the Turks returned to their ship with their cap-tives, they took the local Danish merchant, stripped him of his clothes, made him put on an old and filthy shirt, and put him in irons. They also fettered the other Danish people, who lay that way for seven days. Then they gave the merchant a bad and graceless sweater to wear and released him from the irons.

After the Turks had done all this, another of their ships ar-rived. This ship, which was crewed by no more than thirty men, had to that point gained nothing. The first group of Turkish pirates agreed to take on this new company, but only on the condition that the newcomers should sail their ship, which

1. The þingmannaleið (literally, parliament man's way") was a traditional Ice-landic unit of distance equal to approximately 23.5 miles (37.5 kilometers).

2. This bizarre, violent assault on a young man the corsairs had already trussed up seems senseless. In the heat of the chase, so to speak, the corsairs be-haved savagely, but this was a securely bound captive. A healthy young man would have represented a valuable commodity. The whole corsair enterprise in Iceland, after all, was based on taking captives to sell into slavery at a profit. This is how the manuscript reads, however. No doubt there were at the time details that explained why the corsairs brutalized the young man in this way (or why those Icelanders who "reliably reported" this event felt compelled to say they did), but it is unlikely we shall ever be able to uncover them. There is no mention anywhere of whether the young man survived his ordeal.

was an older ship, into the harbor first and so receive any shot, whether it would be on the Westman Islands or elsewhere. And if that ship was sunk, the first group of pirates agreed to have their own ship nearby so that survivors could be rescued. But the third ship, which was their admiral's, should sail south of the islands, and put ashore there all the raiders.

When these Turkish murderers came abreast of Eyjafjallajökull glacier, they surprised an English fishing vessel with its lines out and captured nine sailors.[3] They spoke calmly to the captain, however, and said that they would give him his men back if he agreed to show them the way to the harbor at the Westman Islands. He agreed to this, having little enough choice, and they set their course.

They reached the Westman Islands early in the day, and stayed off the shore until evening. Around six o'clock, they wanted to set course directly for the harbor. But one of the nine fishermen who had been captured—an Icelander named Þorsteinn—said that he could show the Turkish captain a better approach, which was to go with all his host of men to the south of the island, where he could point out a way to come ashore safely.

The Danish merchant on the Westman Islands had by this time become aware of the presence of the Turkish ships. He set a watch every night on the islands and ordered that all cannons should be cleaned and loaded and ready. He gave every able man a gun. And so the people were ready to defend the harbor.

Once the Danish merchant realized that the Turkish pirates had snuck around southwards of the island instead of entering into the harbor, he rode out on a horse to see if he could make out what they intended to do. When he came to

3. Eyjafjallajökull (pronounced "Eh-ya-fiat-la-yer-kult") refers both to the glacier and to the volcano under that glacier.

the shore, he saw that the Turks were in a great hurry to launch three boats full of people, what seemed to him to be no less than two hundred men at least. Seeing all this, the merchant sent a messenger in haste to the captain of the merchant's ship, instructing him to come with muskets and men to prevent the pirates from making land.

The Turks first tried to land at what is called Kópavík. They did not trust themselves to that shore, however, because of the steep hill there and the rocks above, and also because they saw people roving there. The Turks then rowed south all the way to Brimurð, as it is called.[4]

The merchant was already there on his horse, and with a few men also who had come south with him, ready to receive the pirates. Some of the men were panic stricken, however, seeing the awful crowd of pirates on their way to the land. These men started to scatter to their wives and children in order to get them away to safety.

As the murderous pirates drew near to the rocky shore at Brimurð, the merchant fired a musket at their forward boat. The pirates only shouted wickedly at him and leaped from their boats onto the strand, one after another. Then they all charged towards the merchant, Lauritz Bagge.

When he saw this, the Danish merchant could wait no longer. He leaped onto his horse and galloped back toward the Danish merchants' houses. As he came onto the road, he encountered his captain, Henrich Thomasson. It seemed to the two of them that they could not resist the swarm of pirates who were already on land. The captain rode with Lauritz back to the village. Once there, he went straight to his ship and bashed a hole in her hull so that she would sink. He opened all the ports

4. The events Kláus Eyjólfsson describes take place on Heimaey. See map 2 for locations on the island.

so the water should flow in more freely. Then he cut all the ropes so that the ship might drift free. The captain then hurried to the cannons in the harbor and drove a nail into each, spiking every one, so that, if the pirates should overtake them, as happened, they could not make use of the cannons.

When all this was done, they saw the Turkish pirates come rushing from the south, shouting and screaming and waving red banners. Then it came to the Danish merchant's mind to escape to the mainland. As it happened, there was still a large fishing boat left floating in the harbor.[5] The merchant boarded this vessel with all his household and set off. The captain, when they passed him, did not want to abandon his ship, though he gave his crew leave to go. They all leaped into the ship's boat and made preparations to escape to Klettsnef.

As the Danish merchant drew away, however, he became greatly upset because the captain was left behind alone, and he returned. By now there were shots coming from the Danish houses. The captain leaped aboard the small ship's boat, and the crew rowed to the vessel in which the merchant Lauritz and his household waited. Then they all rowed away as fast as they could towards the mainland in the fishing boat because the Turkish pirates' ship was by then approaching the harbor.

When the fishing boat came out of the sheltered harbor into the open sea, they almost perished, for the wind blew so strongly from the east that they were nearly swamped. They only saved themselves by bailing the seawater out with their caps. By taking a great risk, they came to the mainland about nine o'clock the next morning, losing their oars and other things when landing.

Now I will describe the behavior of the murdering pirates, those wretched dogs.

5. Other sources tell us that this was a ten-oared fishing boat.

First, they scattered around all the island so that nobody should escape. When they came to the town, they drove live-stock and everything before them to the Danish houses at the harbor. That part of their force which, on the way to the town, came to Landakirkja church, surrounded the church, shooting and hewing it with axes until they broke in. First they stole the vestments and dressed themselves up. Then they trooped away from there, driving everyone they captured towards the Danish houses. Those who could not move as fast as the pirates wished, they beat to death and left lying behind. So bloodthirsty were they that they turned back to hack and strike the dead for the sick pleasure of it—as will be described more precisely.

In the inhabited district, they came to Ofanleiti steading. There they captured the Reverend Ólafur Egilsson, along with two maidservants and a baby. When the priest tried to resist, they kicked him and struck him. As he comforted himself, and said that such things he would not have to suffer in another world, they became furious and beat him and his children violently, driving them towards the Danish houses. Before they left Ofanleiti, they first went to Ofanleiti farmstead, where they sought so closely for captives that they lit torches and searched in every house. When they found one old woman hiding atop a pile of firewood, they lit a fire and pulled her off and brought her to Ofanleiti, where they left her lying on the grassy slope in front of the farmhouse while they continued to search round about.

When the eleven-year-old son of Reverend Ólafur Egilsson came by, all unsuspecting, to see his parents, the pirates captured him at once and tied his arms behind his back. He, too, was left outside the farmhouse. The boy asked the old woman to untie him, but she said that she did not dare to do it. When the Turks came out from searching the farmhouse, they checked to see if he was still tied. They had captured two other children of about six years old, whom Reverend Ólafur had taken in. When all this was done, they drove everyone, children and adults, towards the Danish houses.

Then they began to set fire to the island's houses. There was a woman there who could not walk, whom they had captured easily. Her they threw on the fire, along with her two-year-old baby. When she and the poor child screamed and called to God for help, the wicked Turks bellowed with laughter. They stuck both child and mother with the sharp points of their spears, forcing them into the fire, and even stabbed fiercely at the poor, burning bodies.

The Turks searched in every corner and in every hole. They rooted about everywhere, like boars, and no rock or cliff stopped them, as the following example proves.

Using ropes, they climbed up to the caves where the fishermen kept their fish, a height of no less than one hundred fathoms. From those caves, they fetched women and children and made them climb down. Those whom they could not capture without a problem, they shot to death. Some of those whom they shot fell from the caves a hundred fathoms, some sixty, some were left where they had been shot, looking as though they were alive.

Among those who crossed the path of the pirates was a man named Bjarni Valdason, who tried to run away. They struck him across the head above the eyes and killed him. When his wife, who had been fleeing with him, saw this, she at once fell across his body, screaming. The Turks took her by her feet and dragged her away, so that the cloth of her dress came up over the head. Her dead husband they cut into small pieces, as if he were a sheep. They took the woman to the Danish houses and threw her in with the other prisoners.

They also chased a pregnant woman who ran away from them as fast as she could, until she lost her baby and fell down dead, the two parts of her separated.

The other priest who lived on the Islands, the Reverend Pastor Jón, fled with his family, wife and daughter, sons and servants, to seek refuge in a cave. He started to read to his people from scripture, to comfort them. But as he was doing this, he heard the pirates' footsteps and said to his wife, "They are come, Margarét." As they were talking, the bloodthirsty pirates entered the cave. When they saw the Reverend Jón, one of the pirates said, "Why are you not home in your church?" Jón replied, "I have been there this morning." The pirate said, "You will not be there tomorrow." He then struck poor Jón a blow across the head. Reverend Jón stretched out his arms and cried, "I commend me to my God!" The pirate struck him again, and Jón said, "I commit me to my Lord Jesu Christo!" His wife crept to the feet of the murdering pirate and held fast to him, thinking that she could sway him from his violence. But there was no mercy. The pirate struck a third blow, and Reverend Jón said, "It is enough! Lord Jesu, into your hands I commend my spirit!" and died. Then the pirates drove the people to the Danish houses. But one small hole was up in the rock above where this happened. Two women hid themselves there, and they heard and saw all these tidings.[6]

Up in the cliffs above Ofanleiti, the pirates found five stout men, whom they fell upon and captured. One of these men was

6. If this is, in fact, an accurate rendering of events rather than an apocryphal story, it remains to be explained how one of these "Turkish" pirates should be able to speak intelligibly to an Icelander, especially since the corsairs needed a German speaker to converse with Reverend Ólafur when they interrogated him aboard their ship. One possible explanation is that it was a Christian renegado who, knowing Icelandic or possibly Danish, could banter thus with Reverend Jón before murdering him. Another possibility is that this story is simply nascent hagiography. As with other aspects of the Tyrkjaránið, we will likely never know for sure.

unmanageable and did not want to let them tie him. Some of the pirates wanted to kill him because they said that they did not want to be delayed. They then caught sight of two girls. When they chased after these girls, they passed over a hill so that one of the girls managed to evade them and return to the bound men. As she approached them, one of the men implored her to untie him, which she did in a hurry. After that, one man untied another. When the pirates returned to fetch them, the men ran off as fast as they could, not daring to look back, scattering in all directions, until they did not see each other. The distance was long, so the Icelanders could climb down the cliff and seek hiding places there.

When the pirates turned back from there, one of them discovered a woman. He took her and lay with her by force. Then he found a horse and rode with her to the Danish houses.

One man, Erlendur Runólfsson, they drove to the edge of a very high cliff. They took him and stripped him and put him there as a target on the edge of the cliff. Then they shot him to death so that he fell one hundred fathoms.

In many places, women lay dead, some stabbed, some cut into pieces in front of their farmhouse doors, left there so disgracefully that their clothes were hauled up to their necks so that they were nakedly revealed where they should not be. One man named Asmus was in his bed, ill. The pirates stuck him so many times that his bedclothes became red with blood.

Once the tumult of the capture had subsided, the Turks started to select from the people imprisoned in the Danish houses—like when fat sheep are chosen from a fold—and to then drive them to the ships.

Since the Reverend Ólafur Egilsson was growing old, and the pirates saw that he was not physically strong, their main captain wanted to leave him behind. But when his wife heard this, she asked him, for God's sake, not to leave her. He said it should be that way, and that he would suffer along with her.

The captured people were squeezed so closely together in the Danish house that one young boy managed to crouch down and crawl in between their legs and slip out through a door and escape, and he has been able to tell how these events occurred.

What happened to the old people who were there is not known with assurance. It is thought by many that they were destroyed by fire. For once they had selected their prisoners, the pirates set fire to all the Danish houses and burned them to ashes, along with everything that was in them. After the pirates' departure, dead people's bones were found there, and roasted bodies.

In total, the Turks captured well over two hundred people from the Westman Islands. But how many they beat or shot to death, people do not know. Just under thirty people have been buried.

Five persons escaped back ashore after the pirates had captured the island's inhabitants. But the pirates recaptured two of them after they returned to land, which the pirates would have done to everyone if those remaining free had not been able to hide themselves, thanks to God's care.

Those who escaped capture and lived have told about how the pirates dealt with the Danish people, which was straight after the pirates came to the islands. They put 232 people in irons all together. But the Danish people had always prayed to God for help with the Icelandic people. And at last, when the pirates went to leave the harbor, it was seen that dead bodies were floating by their ship, having been thrown overboard by the Turks.[7]

7. Kláus Eyjólfsson seems to be implying here that the "Turkish" corsairs specifically targeted the Danes, killed them, and tossed their bodies overboard into the harbor. This seems unlikely. The Icelandic text is unclear, though, and it is not certain what exactly he means.

Before they departed, the pirates returned to the Landakirkja church and set fire to it and burned the building to ashes.

I cannot truly record here with any justice the disgraceful
events that occurred, save to say that no such terrible thing has
ever been done, neither abroad nor within Iceland, to a defense-
less and harmless people, not even, perhaps, in the destruction
of Jerusalem.

What else is there to do but ask God for mercy?

This has Kláus Eyjólfsson Lögréttumaður [member of the
Lögrétta] written in July of the year 1627.

---

Kláus Eyjólfsson (1584–1674), who lived in Hólmar í Landeyar
in southern Iceland, was a member of the Lögrétta, (the legislature of the Icelandic parliament) and a Lögsagnari (deputy
sherriff) for the Westman Islands in 1635. His father was Eyjólfur Egilsson, brother of Reverend Ólafur Egilsson. As can be
gleaned from the text, Kláus Eyjólfsson wrote his report in July
1627, very soon after the "Turkish" raid, based on accounts from
firsthand witnesses.

# Guðríður Símonardóttir

Letter from Guðríður Símonardóttir, written in the Barbari to her husband, Eyjólfur Sölmundarson, of the Westman Islands, 1635.

MAY THE BLESSINGS of God the Father, the redemption of the Lord Jesus Christ, and the consolation and illumination of the Holy Spirit be always with you, my virtuous master and true husband, Eyjólfur Sölmundarson! May the love of our God support you, body and soul, and may eternal salvation in God be yours! I kiss your hands with my love and think warmly of you, wishing that you shall be happy and blessed in God, and that, through His grace, you may prosper in all things temporal, that you may receive strength to bear the burdens you must, and that, in your leaving of this world, you find eternal peace and goodness in the service of Jesus Christ. Amen.

My dear true husband! Even though I, poor person, would wish with all my heart to be with you and to share again in your prosperity, which may God maintain for you, it looks impossible, for I and those like me are forgotten—we slaves here in the Barbari are the sort of creatures which nobody cares about. May our God grant us his holy affection. And may God give you prosperity, happiness, peace, and a long, good life.

I thank you in tender love and in friendliness for your faithfulness and honesty, and for being to me an honest husband. I ask God to reward you with temporal and spiritual blessings, and I want always to pray, as your true wife in love, that God keep you in His hands and under His protection all the days of your life, because, as we know, there are great perils in this world. May the Lord keep us steady until the end! What I first wish to say about my poor life is that I survive mainly through God's mercy and special benefaction. I am here in the Barbari, and in a Turkish place which is named Arciel [Algiers], with a Turk who bought me and my poor child upon my arrival, which both made me sorrowful and happy. In my distress, under this burden God has justly laid upon me, I become more sad every day to know our son to be in such difficulties and danger. We all must suffer because of our sins, but I am glad, in God, in part....

Guðríður Símonardóttir (1598–1682) wrote this letter to her first husband, Eyjólfur Sölmundarson, a fisherman on the Westman Islands. The letter, of which only the portion translated here remains, came to the bishop of Skálholt, Gísli Oddsson, in 1635; nobody knows when the letter was actually written or how long it took to reach him. The indications are that this letter was probably not written by Guðríður herself, but was written for her by some lettered person.

In 1636—one year after the date of this letter and nearly a decade after her original capture—Guðríður Símonardóttir returned to Iceland. She was one of only thirty-five Icelanders who were successfully ransomed, only twenty-seven of whom ever reached their homes. Upon her return, Guðríður learned that her husband, Eyjólfur, had drowned while fishing off the Westman Islands. She eventually married Hallgrímur Péturs-son, who became a priest and the most admired psalm poet in Iceland. Hallgrímskirkja church in Reykjavík is named in memory of him.

A page from Guðríður Símonardóttir's letter

Guðríður Símonardóttir is a prominent figure in Icelandic folklore and literature. Famous for the contradictions in her life, as a slave in a Muslim country and as the influential wife of an Icelandic priest and psalm poet, she has been the subject of both scholarly and fictional works.

# Guttormur Hallsson

Letter written by Guttormur Hallsson to his children and friends, delivered from the land of the Turks to Iceland Anno 1631.

TO MY DEAR FRIENDS, God's children all, who read these words, I, Guttormur Hallsson, wish you peace, luck, and prosperity. May the living God, His son Jesus Christ, and the Holy Spirit reside with you forever and ever. Amen.

Now, even though I have been so slow to write you, my dear friends in God, I live in hope that this small letter of mine shall come into the hands of my brothers and sisters, especially my good friends in South Múlasýsla, in the east and south of Iceland, namely, Reverend Höskuldur Einarsson from Eydalir and his dear brothers, and Reverend Gizur Gíslason from Múli in Skriðdalur valley.

Firstly, I must let you know that almighty God, in His great power and glory, has preserved my life and wonderfully protected me, body and soul, by His fatherly care, His name be praised and honored for ever and ever. Amen.

I now wish, in a few brief lines, to make known to you how I and my fellow countrymen have fared until now.

As you know, I was captured and taken from my native soil on the 6th day of July, in the year of our Lord 1627. After the Turkish pirates had gathered up me and my poor fellows, they sailed to the south and the Westman Islands, where they viciously attacked the inhabitants, like bloodthirsty wolves over-running carrion. They burnt the buildings, tortured and killed many of the people, and took away all the captives they could, like cruel hunting hounds. But you no doubt know all about this, for these terrible events must be common knowledge in Iceland by now.

From the Westman Islands, the Turkish pirates put to sea on the 20th of July, and both the mainland of Iceland and islands disappeared behind us.

There were three ships, with a total of 400 Icelandic people onboard. We had following winds both night and day for over three weeks, until we came here to this alien land on the 12th of August.[1] The name for this country is Arabia. The part where we were taken is known as Barbaria. The town where I am is called Arigiel or Arsiel [Algiers].

During the voyage here we had a miserable and wretched time. We Icelanders were tossed about from one place to another, and each had almost to lie atop another in the ballast. The ship I was on seemed to hold a hundred people, both young and old. Such a wailing and lamenting was to be heard from the poor souls as would have amazed you. Two women passed away on that ship: the wife of Rafn and a woman from Gautavík. The pirates hurled an old woman from Búlandsness alive into the sea. Two more people died upon arrival here at the Barbari. Two others of those captured with me also have died: Reverend Jón and Katrín. But others of his people live. Of the rest that I know about (with the exception of Jón Egilsson and Jón the carpenter), few of those captured in the east of Iceland have died. But God alone knows what they have suffered.

1. The July 20 date for the corsairs' departure from Iceland matches that given by Reverend Ólafur (and other sources). The August 12 date for arrival in Algiers differs from Reverend Ólafur's date, which was August 16 or 17. This discrepancy is likely explained either by faulty human memory or by Guttormur's arriving as a captive on a different ship and so on a different date.

We spent an entire week after our arrival at Algiers imprisoned there. Crowds of people came to see us, for to them we
were a rare type of people. Many of the heathen women there,
both black and white, had pity on us, shaking their heads and
shedding tears. Some of them gave the children bread; some
gave small coins. Thereafter, we were little by little brought out
to the marketplace, as sheep are sold.

The first choice went to the king. By tradition, he owns
the right to an eighth part of those captured. After that, the
remaining prisoners were led to the street in the market where
Christian captives are sold. But nobody there wanted to buy,
because they thought we were a foolish, weak, and ignorant
people. Moreover, we did not have any skills for the hard labor which this land demands. Also, they knew, which is very
true, that nobody would trouble to buy us from here, because
they would not find any silver for ransom payments in our poor
home country, and so we would be obliged to live here all our
lives and be their slaves until our deaths. They call us "bestial."
But we know more than they, God be thanked.

We were sold and separated from each other with many a
sorrowful cry and scream of pain, so that no one knew what had
happened to another until time had passed and people gradually became acquainted with what had gone on and where everybody was.

There is a great difference here between masters. Some captive slaves get good, gentle, or in-between masters, but some un-
fortunates find themselves with savage, cruel, hardhearted tyrants, who never stop treating them badly, and who force them
to labor and toil with scanty clothing and little food, bound in
iron fetters, from morning till night. Many have had to endure
unfair beatings. God in heaven alone knows all that we Christian people have had to suffer here in this terrible place at the

hands of these vicious criminals. I will say no more of this now. Our Lord knows of the wickedness that transpires in this town. There is nothing here except fear and fright, grumbling and quarrel, murder and manslaughter, haughtiness and arrogance and demoniacal possession, day after day. It may truly be said that we live here in earthly torments, but that God, because of His great mercy, graciously helps us in our struggle.

There are all kinds of people here in the Barbari. First there are those of the Turkish race; then there are Moorish North African people, and the black people, and each have their own language. Then next is the Jewish people, and then those who have been Christian but have renounced their faith. There are also captured Christian people from many countries, especially many hundreds from Spain and France, from Germany, England, Holland and Denmark, Italy, Greece, India, and other smaller countries, islands, and remote areas. There are so many different kinds of languages that I cannot begin to explain them.

I have a Turkish man as my master, an elderly man, but his wife is very young, and they have four children, all young. They have both been gentle with me, especially the wife, so that I have neither been beaten nor insulted. When my master has shouted rebukes at me—the Turks are quick to anger—his temper has subsided due to his wife's kind interventions. May God be praised! Great mercy has God shown towards me in my difficulties here in this alien country, supporting me daily.

When I first came to this land, after I had been here for two weeks, I fell sick with an ague that lasted almost five weeks. I was in great distress because this is not a good place for sick people. Once I recovered enough strength and could walk a little, I was set to work ploughing fields by hand with a tool called a *sappa* which is run over the ground to break up the earth—a custom in this country. I had to walk to and from home daily, in bad weather and good, a distance about twice that between two farms.[2] But God so supported me step by step that it became easy for me.

The hardest time in this country, when the labor is most difficult, is from the winter moon in November (the first month of winter) until the seventh week has passed of summer. During the rest of the year, when I am not ploughing, I must walk the town selling water, which is a difficult labor and one that many Christian people must endure. We must pay our masters a certain amount of money every day. If we can get more than that amount, it is to our profit, and we can use it to feed and clothe ourselves. But if we cannot earn the required amount, then it is taken out of our clothing and our food. Oh, God, how miserable we are in this terrible place.

Many men claim to have suffered here, but for the women the suffering is perhaps worse because these devil people pursue the women and try to force them to renounce their God and Creator. But God has supported many women in this struggle gloriously, so that they have kept their right belief until now, for which God be praised.

Women cost more here than men. Youngsters cost more than the adults. My master gave 60 dalers for me. For some, 10 dalers were given; for some 200; 400 for others; 150, or 58, or 40, or 30 for others. Many Christians from other countries cost 50, 60, or 70 dalers.[3]

There is great distress here for those of us who have been captured. And though we must all admit before men and God, my brothers, that we are sinners and deserving of punishment

2. The "distance between two farms" is not an exact measurement, but it is not exceptionally far, somewhere around a mile, or a little more, perhaps.

3. The "daler" here is the same Danish rigsdaler that Reverend Ólafur uses to quote prices. Compare these prices with the ransom mentioned by Reverend Ólafur in chapter XI: "to ransom my wife and my children … [t]he Turks demanded a total of twelve hundred dalers."

from almighty God, yet in His mercifulness He has been lenient with us. We must thank God for adversity and prosperity, both. I now ask of all those who read these words of mine that you pardon my faults and wickedness, that you forgive any hurt or insult I may have caused to you, and that you pray for me and the other true Christian people here so that God, in His great kindheartedness, may hear you and free us from these cruel tyrants, for He may be the source of salvation when there is no salvation before our eyes. Against almighty God, no man may stand.

At present, my beloved brothers and sisters in God, there is no visible hope of freedom for any of us here. We are poverty-stricken exiles a very long way from our own country, and the wealthy lords of our land are not moved by pity to help redeem us. Now, "for everything there is a season," and God knows well our suffering. He will receive me and my true brothers and sisters in Christ and admit them to the glory of heaven. And though we have been cruelly taken from you, I believe our reunion in the heavenly life to come will be all the more joyful. May God be praised for ever and ever. Amen.

Many things have been taken from us, my blessed brothers, but we comfort ourselves through our Lord, because our salvation is in the hands of God, who created Heaven and Earth. We shall not despair, although it is difficult. Now, we must endure and wait and submit to what God wants, for we are His, body and soul.

I have been most neglectful in not having written you earlier to let you know about our condition here. And now there is some doubt whether this letter will ever reach you because Christian ships do not want to come here, except for some few ships which come with trade from Italy, though there is small advantage for us in their arrival.

Many captured Christian people gain their freedom when their relatives, friends, or acquaintances pay ransom for them. The money is sent on these merchant ships which come here from Italy, because these ships have permission to sail and trade hereabouts. The pirates of the Barbari do not attack them. But everything else the pirates can get, they take: ships, goods, and people. Since I have been here, two and a half years now, the pirates have taken more than 120 ships with goods and people, German, English, Dutch, French and Spanish, so that the Turks have become rich in ships and captives.[4] And they become ever more ferocious and eager as they gain more through their piracy.

The Turks think it is their destiny, one of great nobleness and fame, to overcome Christian people, to rob, murder, and destroy, and so to weaken the base of the Christian religion.

They address us as "devils" and "Christian dogs." Oh, my good friends! This is no child's game here. It is a terrible distress upon us, and a heavy burden. The Lord places upon us a heavy burden, says the holy David, and the Lord helps us to carry it. The Lord is merciful, patient, and kindhearted, and He will enfold all those who are downtrodden, oppressed, and those who suffer injustices.

The Turks are ungodly and wicked: in their conduct and costume, in their fastidiousness and haughty arrogance—all on a daily basis. The Turkish chieftains assume themselves to be as selected vessels of their god, and that no man on earth is worthy enough for them to bow down their head gear and give any

4. Since the Icelanders arrived in Algiers in August 1627, two and a half years would make the date on which Guttormur is writing somewhere in 1630. The introduction to his letter says, "delivered from the Barbari to Iceland Anno 1631." It may be that the letter was written in 1630 but only sent in 1631, or only received in 1631. Or Guttormur got his dates confused, possibly. Or the copyist who penned the introduction to the letter may have been the one confused. There is no straightforward way to resolve this.

reverence or veneration to. They have a special headgear and dress, unlike any other nation's, as are their houses of prayer.

In their meeting houses [mosques], they stand very boldly. If any Christian man walks into one of these houses, he is at once taken and burned on a bright fire. If a Christian man speaks to a Turk, he is quickly arrested, tied to a horse's tail, and pulled to the place of execution, and there burnt or put on racks. Many Christians have been tortured and executed very hideously here since I arrived. God preserve all right-thinking people from such sudden and monstrous death.

There is no news here from other countries other than disturbance and the tidings of war, each nation against another, each realm against another, and even within each country, only fighting and conflict and betrayal. Oh, God! How great a plague it is to be here. May the Lord come soon and make an end to this sinful world. We are in a storm, and the waves break across this world. Oh, Lord, help us cross this perilous ocean, and let us reach to the further land, that eternal land beyond the distress and misery of this wretched and uncertain life. Amen.

Here is a list of those of the people from East Iceland that I know about who live: Rafn Magnússon; Brandur Arngrímsson; Guðmundur Þorsteinsson; two Þorsteins, the siblings from Hamar, where four were captured; the sisters and brothers from Núpur; Stefán Hafliðason; Valdi; Kolbeinn and his wife; Einar Magnússon; Þórey and Steinunn from Háls; Jón Hallsson; Þórður; and Starri. All are "bearing the burden of the day" with great difficulties and distress and still holding their true faith, although many of the women have been pursued and harassed. But God's grace and charity have helped them to withstand these heathenish attacks. God be praised! I ask you all, women and men, brothers and sisters, friends and relatives, to wish all these poor children of God peace and fortune, blessings and joy, prosperity both temporal and eternal from our loving God, His sweet son Jesus Christ, and the Holy Spirit, that Holy Trinity in which we shall dwell, body and soul, forever. Amen.

I now ask you all for God's benediction, that communion of peace which our Lord Jesus Christ has laid between us, sealed and confirmed. Preachers, parents, relatives, friends, brothers, sisters, and all our true Christian fellows from other parts of Iceland, please pray for us to the living God in your daily prayers, that God may have pity on us and rescue us from this yoke of slavery that the ungodly and wicked tyrants have placed upon us, if it is not asked against His merciful will. We are like the prodigal son who squandered his inheritance and did not return to his father's house until hunger and need drove him to it. Oh, Father, look upon us mercifully. Help us, God, and bring us salvation, because of your glory and great name, and forgive us our sins. Amen.

I have many things to write you about, my dear and beloved brothers, if there would be time, but this letter must be of few words for now because I do not know if it will ever reach you. It must first go by way of Italy; after that, I do not know what may happen to it. My dear good friends, I have written this hurriedly, pouring out everything, to let you know how things stand with me and those along with me.

Only God's charity has sustained us, miserable and ignorant as we are, in this alien country, for which may His holy and highly blessed name be praised for ever and ever. Amen.

Guttormur Hallsson, by his own hand.

Your poor fellow under God's mercy, captured in Djúpivogur in the Eastfjords of Iceland.

*Post scriptum—*

God shall determine, my beloved sisters and brothers in God, whether I will be ever able to write to you again, but please remember me in your daily prayers. I salute you with tears and a kiss of love. All our names shall be written in the "book of life" in the Lord's hand, until we later will see each other and live together in eternal heavenly glory and joy with God, His blessed angels, and the select for all eternity. May God be praised for ever and ever. Amen.

Written during the night in a hidden place in the capital here in Barbari which is named Argiel or Arsciel [Algiers] on the 20th of November, in the year of our Lord 1631.

Oh! What great comfort I would get, my dear brothers, if you would, for God's sake, send me a letter, so that it could come the same way here to me that this letter has to you. Perhaps it may be carried by some pious men in Denmark or Hamburg, who sail to Italy and to that renowned place Livorno, where merchants come together from many countries, for the merchants there have license to sail to this place and to trade here. It is scarcely a week's sail from there to here. It would give me great joy to hear from you, if it be God's will.

These bastard pirates are planning to voyage to Iceland again, but they wait to see if any ransom will be paid for those of us already here, because if the "payment of freedom" comes here for us, they do not care about anything else.

Blessed God is our refuge, and in His merciful hands we remain. May God preserve our poor country from such grim and ruthless oppression, and from bitter and sudden death. Amen.

Guttormur Hallsson lived and worked on Búlandsnes farm, south of Djúpivogur, in eastern Iceland.

Among those captured in eastern Iceland was Guttomur's farmhand, Jón Ásbjarnarson. An intelligent and energetic young man, Jón became popular among upper-class Muslim society in Algiers and used his status to help his fellow Icelanders. He bought Guttormur's freedom in 1634 and sent him back home with a considerable sum of money (about 100 dalers).

As the ship Guttormur was travelling on drew close to England, four of the crew robbed him, killing him in the process, and tossed his body overboard. When the ship docked, two of the murderers were captured and hanged. The other two escaped. We know of these events because, in 1635, an English fishing vessel brought to Iceland a letter from the captain of the ship on which Guttormur had been murdered. This letter told of Guttormur's death and explained that his effects were stored in Bristol, in England, and would be confiscated by the local authorities if Guttormur's relatives did not retrieve them. There is no record of whether or not they were ever retrieved.

# Jón Jónsson

Letter by Jón Jónsson, who was captured from Grindavík, written from the Barbari to his parents in Iceland in 1630.

MAY THE ETERNAL and merciful Lord God, our revered and beloved redeemer the Lord Jesus Christ, with help and support from the Holy Spirit, that glorious high Holy Trinity, give you mercy, peace, blessings, and long life, and may He provide for you and embrace you now and forever, our parents, our good father, Jón Guðlaugsson, and loving mother, Guðrún Jónsdóttir.

From the depths of our hearts, we, your poor sons, thank you both for the charity, kindness, and love you have shown us, in the name of God, the source of greater grace than we can wish, and of all blessings and benedictions, body and soul. Amen.[1]

We ask you now to forgive, in the name of God, our childhood disobediences, our unruliness and our faults, for we would wish to be included in your warm prayers and intercessions unto God, trusting that our deserved exile and proscription will end well, since the parents' blessing builds the children a house. We see here daily indications of God's mercy, and perhaps your prayers too, for we have kept our Christian faith, and we are

1. Jón is writing on behalf of himself and his brother Helgi. Both men were enslaved in Algiers.

together in one city, not far off from each other, and see each other almost daily. In this, God's mercy has rewarded us, for which He should have eternal thanks. We also have been healthy since our separation happened. I have twice had the ague, but have recovered well.

Many distressing things have happened during our days here, which we used to pass in coldness and hunger and thirst, ill clothed and in great difficulties. But all that is now forgotten, for our masters treat us much better since we have learned to understand the language here and so can defend ourselves against their harsh and aggressive words.[2] The hardest test is over, thanks to the mercy of the Holy Spirit—namely the temptation to forsake our holy Christian faith. And thanks to the glorious work of God, all has gone well for us here, and we have suffered neither blow nor beating. Though there are many evil men here, like demons incarnate, they have not been able to touch us, nor most of our fellow countrymen.

I have not written to the king [of Denmark] because we Icelanders here believe our king will show his mercy to us and save us, as has been told to us many times. We live in expectation of this, and the Turks themselves anticipate ransom for us; therefore, they have not sought to capture more people from Iceland. And we expect that Reverend Ólafur [Egilsson] or the letters he has written may aid in our rescue from these evil men.[3]

The way from here is very long and difficult, however. The merchant ships from Livorno, in Italy, which anchor here with their wares, cannot depart when they want, for their sails are kept inside the city by the Turks. Last year, during a war among the Turkish devils themselves, a Christian ship was kept here

2. When Jón wrote this letter, the captive Icelanders had been enslaved for just under two and a half years.

3. Any letters Reverend Ólafur may have written on behalf of the captive Icelanders have disappeared.

and had to spend its money for food for a full six months. This, and other difficulties, means that few letters get taken. And those who live in Denmark or Norway, and are ransomed from here, do not take letters with them. I think perhaps that Jaspar, from the Westman Islands, could have told news of me, that I am here in the Barbari, in the town where he was. But he left here so suddenly that I did not know until he was already on-board the ship. My writing to you was also hindered because I wrote a letter for Jón, son of Reverend Jón, now deceased, to his brothers, and the country sheriff, Mr. Gísli Hákonarson, because Jón's cruel master did not allow him to write a long letter.[4] Everybody knows everybody else's business here; therefore, men have to sneak away to write in secret when the rest are sleeping.

The late Bjarni Ólafsson, who is now dead, and Jón Þórðar-son came here from the town of Salé. Jón, our uncle, is still in that town. He works as a ploughman for a merchant there, and his master is the best in all that town. Helgi, my brother, went from here to the town of Salé with his master. He met our brother Héðinn and asked him how our mother was do-ing, and whether she was well and healthy. But Héðinn replied that she had gone away, and our dear Halldór with her, too, as well as what was left of the people, and Héðinn started to cry, for he had not been allowed to go, although a great sum of pay-ment had been offered for him.[5] Helgi said that he had advised

4. The "Reverend Jón, now deceased" mentioned here is the Reverend Jón Þor-steinsson, the pastor at Kirkjubær parish on the island of Heimaey, who was mur-dered during the corsair raid. Jón Jónsson the murdered reverend's son (c.1612–49), led an adventurous life. In Icelandic history he is called Jón Vestmann, and he is among the best known of all the Icelandic captives. In Algiers, he "turned Turk," ad-vanced to the rank of a corsair captain, was captured by the Spanish, was ransomed (though his crew were all hung), then made his way from Spain to France and, eventually, to Copenhagen, where he became an officer in the Danish Royal Navy. The letter Jón wrote for Jón Jónsson (Jón Þorsteinsson's son) has disappeared.

5. This account needs a little clarification. Jón was captured, along with his

Héðinn to volunteer to be a galley slave, because that way he could most likely be saved later, which quite often happens.[6] God's grace enlightens our souls and touches our hearts. Now, the doom of the Lord falls upon the children of God, and the words of the Lord run as follows: "Let them do as they can." This is the reign of the power of darkness. Oh! Lord and master of Heaven and Earth, great and all-powerful God, you know best how your will shall be done, that evil men might have dominion over your own children and uproot them, branch and twig. Oh! My brothers, it would have been better for you if you had been one of the children of Bethlehem. They shall suffer retribution, those who have tormented you and pushed you from the road. But God shall be merciful towards you, because his mercy is everywhere.

*An necis longas regibus esse manus?* [Do you not know that kings have long arms?][7]

My brother Helgi has had many masters. His master here in this town is a Greek renegade who has abandoned his reli-

---

two brothers, Helgi and Héðinn, his mother, two of his uncles, Jón and Halldór, and a dozen or so others, in Grindavík by the first set of corsair raiders, a different group from the one that attacked Heimaey and abducted Reverend Ólafur and his family. The Grindavík captives were taken to Salé, on the Atlantic coast of what is now Morocco, and sold into slavery there. Jón and his brother Helgi wound up in Algiers, but the other Grindavíkers remained in Salé. Jón's mother, his uncle Halldór, and some of the other Icelanders were successfully ransomed, in a private arrangement brokered by a Dutchman, and returned to Iceland in 1628 (two years before Jón wrote this letter). Jón's brother Héðinn, however, remained behind in Salé, seemingly because his owner refused the ransom offered for him. The first Jón heard about any of this, apparently, was when his brother Helgi visited Salé "with his master" and returned to Algiers with the news.

6. It is not clear in what way Héðinn might "most likely be saved later" as a galley slave. Perhaps Jón means that there is a chance that any corsair galley on which Héðinn labored might be captured by a ship from a Christian country and the slaves thus liberated. If this is indeed what he means, asserting that such capture and liberation "quite often happens" seems like wishful (or desperate) thinking.

7. Ovid, Heroides 17.186. "Necis" should read "nescis."

gion and is now a chief over many soldiers. From the beginning, Helgi's master tried every way, through beatings and threats, to turn Helgi from the true faith. But in the end Helgi said to his master, "If you do not stop beating and bullying me, you will be searching for silver payment for me in the sea. For I shall throw myself from the castle and die there, rather than deny my true God!" His master's attitude softened when he heard these words, and he has not pressured Helgi or beaten him since.

There was a woman here whom they stripped the clothes from and burned at a stake. Some people here have been hung up by their feet and whipped with ropes, but have managed to defend themselves so that many have survived, thanks be to God. Praised be His holy name for ever and ever. Amen. There are many people here who have been forced to turn from the true Christian religion, may God forgive them. The people here are also distressed by heavy, hard labor and grim circumstances.

I have been sold five times. This latest time, I cost my new master 457 *döblur* (but four döblur convert to a real, which we call a *dei*, so one döbla equals a Danish *mark*). It is most difficult for those who are bought and sold here at such great expense to gain their freedom, because it is impossible for them to earn enough money to buy that freedom for themselves. My master now says that he wants over 800 döblur for me.[8] There is also the city tax, the port tax, and the king's tax. It is impossible to escape from here to Oran, which is a Christian town. It is fifty Spanish miles from here, and, in between, there are numerous Moorish towns.[9] The moors get twenty dalers when

8. See the discussion at the end of this letter for details about the ransom prices Jón mentions.

9. At this time Oran was occupied by the Spanish, hence it was a "Christian town." The "Spanish mile" Jón mentions is likely the *legua de por grado* (league of the degree), which could equal between 4.5 and 4.8 statute miles (7.32–7.86 kilometers), depending on how it was measured. Fifty such Spanish miles would

they can capture escaped slaves. Those they recapture are tied by their masters to a wooden post and flogged on their naked bodies. Afterwards, they are manacled in iron chains. After being so chained up, they are helpless to escape again.

If one knows the language of the Moors, or the Arabian language, then he can well come through all manner of hindrances here. I heard of a Portuguese man who wore Arabian dress and tried to walk to Oran. He would enter into the Moorish churches [mosques] every evening. When he was no more than two days journey from Oran, he entered as before into one of these Moorish churches. But when he bent over for the fifth time with them, a small crucifix and copper Peter [a talisman made of copper], which hung on a string of rosary beads around his neck, fell out of his robe. When they saw this, the Moors beat him and placed him in iron fetters and dragged him back here, worse than dead.

There are some captured people here who sneak boats into the forest and eventually escape in them. Some people grow too ambitious, though, and attempt to construct large, eight- oared boats able to hold many passengers. Often, they are not able to finish building such big vessels. Some neglect to place lookouts in the trees to watch for coming people, to ensure that the sounds of the hammers will not be heard. Those who neglect this are caught and suffer terribly. If they take boats from the merchant ships from Livorno which lie at harbor here, the merchant ship, the crew, and the cargo are all at risk. And if the crew of a ship is discovered trying to hide an escaped slave—for the Turks inspect the ships when a slave is missing—then the ship and crew and all are forfeited and become the property of

---

equal between 225 and 240 statute miles (362–386 kilometers). The overland distance between Algiers and Oran is about 250 statute miles (402 kilometers). For a discussion of seventeenth century measures of distance, see Currencies and Distances in the Icelandic Background section of the Appendixes.

the Turkish king. Therefore, the sails of the ships are kept by the Turks, and the boats are tied fast to the ships.

So there is very little possibility of escape from this place, unless God himself should choose to intervene—which does happen. Therefore, it is best to wait for a moment when God offers an opportunity.

Most of the Christian captives here are from Spain, Portugal, and Galicia [in northwest Spain]. Many are also French, either under King Philip of Madrid in Spain, or from Marseilles. Some are from Slavonia [in the Balkans] and from Italy, but very few are from the Nordic countries.

The king of Spain wanted to sail with his galleon and other great ships of war to rescue all the captives here by force of arms. But it is said, in truth, that the king is afraid of a devilish wizard here who has, once before, broken the king's fleet with a violent storm. The king's fleet suffered such terrible damage that only his own ship and that of his admiral survived.

All this came about because of the king's own greed. When he had conquered the place, he had a castle built, which is now in ruins, and he demanded the keys to the gates of the town. The inhabitants offered him the keys of the town, but the king was not satisfied and wanted keys of precious gold to be delivered to him within three days.

The wizard had meanwhile been preparing himself with his secret magical skill. He walked to the port and threw into the sea a small drum with magical characters inscribed on it. Then the sea started to toss and was suddenly gripped by a powerful storm with waves so strong that one Spanish ship was driven against another, and they were broken all to pieces. The king of Spain's crown was thrown into the sea, and, to this day, it is kept here in the town's treasury. Therefore, the people from Spain say that the king of Madrid only has half his crown on the front of his head, and that he has vowed to return to the Barbari to seek his lost crown.[10]

Since the big punishment began to be meted out on the wicked inhabitants of these towns for their villainy, they have rioted among themselves, because the sons of the renegades, who here are called *kardooleis,* have wanted to take over the town from the Turks and make it their own, and the Turks' masters make war secretly against the Tremesen, who belong to this king's town, so the Turks and they were fighting over possession of the town. Because of this, the Turks became so cautious that they walked with unsheathed daggers and swords under their coats into their churches. The kardooleis concealed their weapons, but the Turks, looking closely, tore the coats off them and discovered the fraud. The Turks were frightened by this and banished the kardooleis from the town. Those who came back, and did not leave within three days, were hung and then thrown into the sea. Their houses were demolished to the ground by iron sledgehammers. Soldiers were needed in Tremesen. Therefore, the Turks sent fifteen big ships to Egypt and Turkey to provide soldiers, so that there are very few people left behind here.[11]

10. Jón seems to be referring here to King Charles V's spectacularly unsuccessful attack on Algiers in October, 1541, in which the Spanish king lost perhaps as many as 150 ships and 12,000 men. As for the wizard that Jón mentions, Father Pierre Dan, the Trinitarian friar who was in Algiers in 1634, relates (in *Histoire de Barbarie,* book 2, chapter 5, section 1) a story of how, when Charles V's army was besieging Algiers, "a famous sorcerer of the city, that history does not name, went to find Assan Aga [Hassan Ağa, commander of the *Ocak,* the Ottoman military garrison of the city] ... and asked him to hold out another nine days, assuring him that, in that time, he would infallibly deliver Algiers from the siege and dissipate entirely the enemy army.... Events happened just as he had predicted ... a storm so furious that fifteen galleys and over a hundred vessels were lost." If Charles V's failed attack is indeed the incident Jón is recounting, it says something, perhaps, about the persistence of oral narrative that Jón, writing in 1630, almost a century after these events, should recount them in such detail, as if they had only recently happened.

11. See the discussion at the end of this letter for more about the kardooleis and Tremesen revolts.

Those who are in Spain know all this because Christian people flee from here daily in boats, and it is said here that the king of Spain has a ship prepared and sixty galleys which are at anchor in Carthage [Tunis], waiting to sail. May God grant them victory. Meanwhile, the Christian people here are put into towers, prisons, and dungeons. But the Turks do not dare to harm anyone, for fear of what may eventually come to pass. God has power enough to aid the helpless.

> Non dubito, nunquam dubitavi, nec dubitabo,
> Num pie nostra queas, Christe, levara mala.
> Sed dubito, num nostra velis mala, Christe, levare;
> Hoc est: an nobis utile id esse putes.
> Ergo voluntati subjecta erit usque voluntas
> Nostra tuae, si vis, Christe, juvare potes.
> Exoptata licet tua nondum venerit hora,
> Illa tamen veniet, quum tibi, Christe, placet.

> [I do not doubt, have never doubted, will never doubt
> That you, Christ, can relieve our misfortunes.
> But I do doubt, Christ, that you might wish to relieve
>    our misfortunes;
> That is, whether you look at such relief as good for us.
> Therefore, our will shall always remain subject to yours.
> If you wish, Christ, you have the power to aid us.
> Although that time is not yet here,
> It shall come to pass when you will it.]

Therefore shall we be glad in hope, patient in our pain, and firm in prayer. God will take care of our necessities, because what one prays for will come to pass. Should any of our sovereign rulers have forgotten, God thus spoke to Esaiam [Isaiah 49:23]: "The kings shall be your foster fathers and the queens your foster mothers." This was decreed without exception. Should kings and lords at once forget all their coronation oaths that they swore by their crown and scepter, when they walked from the altar of God, to uphold His justice? For they rule by God's will, and they should be just and righteous shepherds to the common people, so that the people may live in peace and happiness. Therefore, it would be an act of great charity, and God's work, if our king were to ransom us, his poor sheep, exiled and under the burden of captivity, as were those under the Pharaohs. In very truth, God will repay all good deeds upon the resurrection of the righteous, as it is written: "What you do to even the least of those who believe in me, that you do to me."

It would bring us such great happiness if we could anticipate aid to free us from here, and it would help us all, myself and others, especially the distressed men and women of Iceland, to endure the days of captivity to come. We pray with hot tears and sighs of grief, as He has ordered in Psalm 50,[12] and in another Psalm (91): "Because he invokes my name, I shall save him," et cetera.

> Sint peritura licet caelumque salumque solumque,
> Verba dei et verbis qui stetit usque manent.
>
> [Although the heaven, the ocean, and the sun perish,
> The words of the Lord, and those who believe in
> them, will remain forever.]

God Himself shall decree how the days of our exile and captivity may pass. Whether we live or die, we are God's, and He is with us till the end of the world; He has counted the hairs of our head, and in His palms are our baptismal names. Thus I say often:

> Herra Jesú mín heillin góð
> sem hefur mig frelsað fyrir þitt blóð

12. Jón is likely referring to Psalm 50:15: "And call upon me in the day of trouble: I will deliver thee, and thou shalt glorify me."

eg bið þig, eðla herra,
greið þú mitt ráð,
gef þú mér ráð.
Guð, lát mitt angur þverra.

Í saurgan getinn er eg einn,
engi maður kann fæðast hreinn
af syndum spilltu sæði,
alið hef eg
minn aldurs veg
í heimsins hryggðaræði

Í dóm við auman þrælinn þinn,
þá ganga viltu herra minn,
þín miskunn góð mér hlífi,
sjá þú eg ber
syndir með mér
sjúkur frá móðurlífi.

Væg þú minn herra veikum mér,
volaður sem þig biður hér
bundinn með Belials hlekkjum;
leys mig og geym
minn guð frá þeim
og grimmum Satans hrekkjum.

Einninn frá vondra illum sið
eilífi guð mér forða bið
að yfirvinna megi
með sigurprís
í Paradís
á efsta dómsins degi.

[Lord Jesus, my fortune,
who has redeemed me with your blood,
I beg you, noble master,
help me on my way,

give me your mercy.
God, let my sorrow disappear.

In sin I am conceived;
no man can be born pure
from sinful seed.
I have lived
all my long years
in this world's sorrows

When you judge your poor slave,
then, my dear Lord,
shield me with your good mercy.
Look, I bear
sins within myself,
sick from my mother's womb.

Have mercy on my weakness,
my dear Lord, a poor soul who asks you,
tied with the devil Belial's chains;
redeem me,
my God, and keep me safe
from Satan's cruel wiles.

Also, from the habits of evil people,
eternal God, I ask you
to save me
so that I may triumph victoriously
in Paradise
on the final Day of Judgment.]

We cannot ask anything from you, our parents, other than what, through righteous prayer, may come to pass for us. God be thanked that our blessed mother was liberated from here. I speak truly for myself, who is here still, knowing that all your money has been used up for her liberation. Now our hope is for charity from our king, because his war has now ended, which he had with the emperor, and we anticipate good news with six Dutch war ships which are supposed to come here to emancipate their people.[13]

Reverend Ólafur Egilsson is gone from here, but Jaspar from the Westman Islands, Andrés from Djúpivogur, and some of his men, including his shopkeeper's assistant, are all waiting here with us. If all this goes wrong or is delayed, I ask you to write to me. Send the letter to Copenhagen, to Lauritz Bentssonar, or to your other acquaintances there. From there, it can go by way of Livorno, in Italy, or Marseilles, in France, and then from there to here. But we live in hope that payment will arrive here from Denmark soon.

There was a man here from Norway, who gave money for the prisoners here in the Barbari at the command of the King of Denmark and Norway. And it has been said that a great sum of tribute is kept in Holland from Denmark. Perhaps it will be that this can be exchanged for us and other prisoners here who are subjects of the Danish King.

Lastly, I want to end this letter by respectfully asking you, my parents, to commend our souls, and those of our relatives and neighbors here, into God's hands. May God bless you both, body and soul, now and forever. As it says in 1 Corinthians 11: "When we are judged, we are chastened of the Lord."

To the honorable Lord Oddur Einarsson, the bishop, and his honest wife, and to his whole household, I wish the best of fortune, and good fortune also to my schoolmasters Jón Gizurarson and Ketill Jörundsson, Reverend Vigfús, Snorri Jónsson, Björn Einarsson and his wife, and the whole school, and the Reverend Oddur, Reverend Grímur, Halldór, and my uncles

---

13. Jón is referring to the Thirty Years' War. "Our king" is Christian IV of Denmark. Denmark withdrew from the Thirty Years' War in 1629. The war itself did not end until 1648.

and all my acquaintances in Grindavík, young and old—I cannot name them all. If my grandparents, Philippus and Hjálmar, are still alive, I wish them all the best, body and soul. Amen.

I witness, by God, that I do not have time to write to either the bishop or Reverend Gísli Bjarnason, whose prayers from the pulpit I would gladly receive, nor to my dear teachers whom I mentioned before, and for that I ask their forgiveness. I do not now live in freedom.

> Heic mihi servitium video labore esse paratum;
> Tu mihi liberas illa paterna, vale.
>
> [Here I see bondage and hard labor;
> Farewell, to you, my former father, my freedom.]

No so fullan para los bastimentos, sino lavansensia de los demas amigos mios. A foderoso sonnar Dios remidiet sus probetis Psclavos.[14]

May the mercy of the Father, the charity of the Son, and the comfort of the Holy Spirit, that holy Trinity, be with you, now and forever, by the blood of Jesus, Mary's son, which washes away all our sins. Amen.

Be victorious in God for ever.

Written in a great haste, during the night when all slept in the land of Barbari, from the town Artzel [Algiers] in the year of our Lord 1630, at the first night of the nine weeks of fasting for Lent, that is the 24th of January.

> Your poor imprisoned sons
> Jón Jónsson and Helgi Jónsson
> Awaiting the Lord's salvation.

14. See the discussion at the end of this letter for more about these intriguing sentences.

There are some aspects of Jón Jónsson's letter that require explication too long for footnotes.

When discussing his situation in Algiers, Jón writes: "I have been sold five times. This latest time, I cost my new master 457 döblur (but four döblur convert to a real, which we call a dei, so one döbla equals a Danish mark).... My master now says that he wants over 800 döblur for me." It is not entirely certain what unit of currency Jón means by "döblur," but he probably intends Algerian money. In *The History of Algiers and Its Slavery*, Emanuel d'Aranda, the Flemish soldier enslaved in Algiers in the 1640s, refers to coins he calls "Morisco doubles." Since döblur means "doubles" in Icelandic, Jón likely has these Morisco doubles in mind. The French version of d'Aranda's text reads as follows: "Le gage des soldats est de huićt doubles Morisques par Lune … châque double vaut douze patars de nostre monnoye." John Davies's translation renders this as: "The pay of the Soldiery is eight Morisco Doubles a month, every Double is worth twelve Patars" (a Flemish coin). Davies's translation also includes a useful parenthetical addition: "every Double is worth twelve Patars (that is somewhat better than twelve pence Sterling)." One "double," then, equaled approximately one English shilling (12 pence to a shilling). In St. John Seymour's *Adventures and Experiences of a Seventeenth-Century Clergyman*, we read that Reverend Devereux Spratt, an English clergyman enslaved in Algiers in the 1640s, was ransomed for 200 "Cobes." A cobe was equivalent to a Spanish real de a ocho, the famous "piece of eight." Spratt's ransom equaled forty English pounds—an exchange rate of four shillings to one cobe/real de a ocho. According to these sources, then, four döblur were equal to one real de a ocho. This matches Jón's assessment ("4 döblur convert to a real") if we assume that by "real" he means real de a ocho.

Ransoms in Algiers were set in a variety of currencies, but frequently they were paid in reales de a ocho, since at the time this was an internationally recognized coin of standard value. The real de a ocho was equivalent to other standard value coins, including the Danish rigsdaler. In chapter XI, for example, Reverend Ólafur writes: "to ransom my wife and my children ... [t]he Turks demanded a total of twelve hundred dalers [i.e., rigsdalers], which they call 'Stück von achten' (German for 'pieces of eight')." Four döblur, then, would equal one rigsdaler. With this four-to-one exchange rate, Jón's 457 döblur ransom would equal a little over 114 rigsdalers; and his 800 döblur ransom, about 200 rigsdalers. These amounts fit reasonably well within the upper and lower limits of the ransom payments made for the Icelandic captives, which ranged from about 45 to around 250 rigsdaler per person.

A ransom amount of 200 rigsdalers/reales de a ocho seems a bit low, though, for a man of Jón's education and obvious worth. As far as we know, he was never ransomed. At the price he seems to quote, one would expect he would have been.

———

Jón mentions two rebellions: "the sons of the renegades, who here are called kardooleis, have wanted to take over the town from the Turks and make it their own, and the Turks' masters make war secretly against the Tremesen, who belong to this king's town, so the Turks and they were fighting over possession of the town."

As it turns out, Father Pierre Dan, the Trinitarian friar who was in Algiers in 1634, describes both these rebellions in his *Histoire de Barbarie*.

Dan renders *kardooleis* as *Coulouglis*. Both terms are variants of *Koulouglis* (also spelled Kouloughlis, Cologhlis, Qulaughlis), a rendering of *kuloğlu* (Turkish *kul*, "servant," and *oğlu*, "son of"), which was the Turkish term for the sons of members of the Ocak born by native Algerian women. The Ocak, a combination of military body, occupying force, and governing council, was the name given to the régime established by the Ottoman Turkish rulers of Algiers. The military arm of the Ocak was composed primarily of janissaries.

Janissaries (from Turkish *yeni çeri*, meaning "new soldier") were formed using the *devşirme* (from Turkish "collecting") system, in which non-Muslim boys living in lands ruled by the Ottoman Empire (such as the Balkans) were taken from their families, converted to Islam, and taught Ottoman language, culture, and military skills. Janissaries functioned initially as a sort of Praetorian Guard for the sultan, but by the seventeenth century they formed a more general core of troops. Since janissaries came originally from Christian lands, they could be viewed by Christians as being renegados—hence Jón's description of the kardooleis as "sons of the renegades."

Most sources agree that only men of Turkish origin were admitted into the Ocak. The Koulouglis were thus excluded. This ban, apparently, is what the Koulouglis were rebelling against. Dan's account is a little confusing, since he asserts that the Koulouglis were indeed part of what he calls the Divan (which he describes as "the State Council, both of the city and the whole kingdom"). There was nothing, however, to prevent Koulouglis from holding high positions in the Algiers equivalent of municipal government and among the city's corsairs, and perhaps Dan was confused about this (though he seems rarely to be confused about anything). Or perhaps the ban was not, in fact, as strict as is supposed. In any case, the Koulouglis clearly felt they were badly done by and resolved to do something about the situation.

Here is an abridged version of Dan's description of the

Koulouglis (Coulouglis) rebellion (from *Histoire de Barbarie,* book 2, chapter 5, section 4).

The Militia that governs the city and the kingdom of Algiers is composed of natural Turks from the Levant, of those from the city and the surrounding area, which they call Coulouglis in their language, that is to say children of the country, and of renegades from all kinds of nations. To this militia accrue the honors and dignities of the kingdom, powerful enticements to animate the courage and ambitions of the militiamen.

Many Coulouglis were involved in the Divan, including being heads of the Militia, and the Coulouglis were so convinced of their powerful alliances and gifts of fortune that they resolved they should be masters of Algiers rather than have the city controlled by foreigners. To this aim, they assembled a large force consisting of more than eighteen hundred people.

In response to this threat, which could conceivably raze the city and ruin the entire state, the high officers of the Divan proclaimed a resolution to expel the Coulouglis and commanded them to leave the city within two days, and the kingdom within a month. This order was published and put into effect about the end of 1629. Many of the Coulouglis, not wishing to put their lives in danger, went elsewhere, but there were others who could not resolve to leave the country entirely, and so hid in some houses outside the city, on the expectation that they would eventually be able to get permission to return to Algiers.

Several months passed, and people spoke no more of the Coulouglis, thinking they had all left the kingdom. During this interval, however, some Coulouglis were recognized in the city, in disguise. They were immediately seized and, as an example, executed by being put in a bag and thrown into the sea. And so it seemed that all memory of them was abolished. But the remaining exiles then began secretly assembling and entered the city, some disguised as Moors, others as women, their weapons hidden under their clothes. They made their way to the Alcassave and made themselves masters of the for- •

tress.[15] The rebels expected that all their relatives and friends would immediately take up arms with them and aid their cause, but no one dared declare for them.

The city Militia assaulted the fortress, some soldiers scaling the walls while others blew open the entrance and stormed inside. Then some of the Coulouglis, realizing they were overwhelmed and that they would be punished for their crimes by the most cruel tortures that could be invented, drew courage from despair and resolved to die with their enemies. As the fortress filled with soldiers, they set alight the powder magazines in the fortress's cellars. The violence of the explosion that ensued was so great that it killed almost all those present and toppled several neighboring houses. More than five hundred were slain in the destruction of the fortress, and more than six thousand— men, women, children, and many Christian slaves—died due to falling debris and the fires that followed.

Those of the rebels who escaped the conflagration were seized immediately and condemned to the most cruel tortures that could be devised.

Jón Jónsson's description of the Koulouglis (Coulouglis) rebellion and Father Dan's do not match exactly, but they overlap sufficiently for it to be clear that both men are describing the same event, especially since the dates coincide so nicely. According to Dan, the rebellion occurred around 1629–30. Jón had been a slave since the autumn of 1627 and dated his letter the 24th of January, 1630. The correspondences between the two men's descriptions are clear. Jón writes: "The kardooleis concealed their weapons, but the Turks, looking closely, tore the coats off them and discovered the fraud. The Turks were

15. Alcassave, cassave, casbah, a qasbah, qassabah, al-qasaba are all variants of *kasbah* (from Arabic *qaṣba*, meaning "citadel"). The Kasbah (Al-Qasaba) of Algiers was located on the heights of the city, built against the apex of the western (inland-facing) wall, and formed a self-contained enclave. It served not only as a fortress and armory, but also as a seat of government where the Divan met.

frightened by this and banished the kardooleis from the town. Those who came back, and did not leave within three days, were hung and then thrown into the sea." Dan writes: "the Divan proclaimed a resolution to expel the Coulouglis and commanded them to leave the city within two days, and the kingdom within a month.... some Coulouglis were recognized in the city, in disguise. They were immediately seized and, as an example, executed by being put in a bag and thrown into the sea. The remaining exiles then began secretly assembling and entered the city, some disguised as Moors, others as women, their weapons hidden under their clothes."

Jón Jónsson makes no mention of the destruction of the Alcassave, which may seem a little surprising at first, since one assumes such a great explosion and its terrible aftermath would be indelibly imprinted on the minds of all who were nearby. Dan's dating is not precise, but it appears quite likely that the storming of the Alcassave and the subsequent explosive destruction of the fortress happened after Jón finished writing his letter. Dan states that the order expelling the Koulouglis was published "about the end of 1629," and that, afterwards, "several months passed" during which a number of disguised Koulouglis were seized and executed by being "put in a bag and thrown into the sea." More time passed (though exactly how much is unclear) before the remaining Koulouglis "began secretly assembling and entered the city." So it is quite possible that while Jón might have heard about the expulsion order and the execution of disguised Koulouglis trying to infiltrate the city, the battle for the Alcassave did not occur until several months into 1630—too late for him to be able to include mention of it in his letter. There is another possibility, however. Francis Knight, an English captive in Algiers, discussed the destruction of the Al-Qasaba fortress in *A relation of seauen yeares slaverie under the Turkes of Argeire* (published in 1640): "in the year 1634, on Friday the 20 of June ... the Cassaba or house of Council, and chief fortress of that City [was blown up]." If Knight has the date right, the Al-Qasaba battle happened well after Jón penned his letter.

———————

Father Dan also describes the Tremesen rebellion.

"Tremesen" is a variant spelling/pronunciation of the city Tlemcen (also spelled Tlemsen, Tlemsan, Tilimsen), located some 320 miles (515 kilometers) west of Algiers but still at that time within the Algerian sanjak, and thus under Ottoman rule.

Here is an abridged version of Dan's description of the Tremesen rebellion (from *Histoire de Barbarie*, book 2, chapter 5, section 2). His original spelling for the city's name, in the seventeenth century orthography, was "Tremeffen." We have rendered that as "Tremesen."

A *marabout* of Tremesen, a town under the rulership of Algiers, became disordered by his ambition, dwelling more on earthly matters than on those of Heaven.[16] This impostor emerged from the cell where he had retired and convinced the leaders of the town of Tremesen that he had received secret revelations from the prophet Mohammed, who was sorry to see their city under the tyranny of Algiers—a city that had once been merely a part of the kingdom of Tremesen, when Tremesen had been the capital of all that country—and had inspired him with the true means to soon shake off the yoke of Algiers' tyrannical rule.

This marabout told the townspeople of Tremesen that Mohammad had vouchsafed to him a particular secret to overcoming their enemies, and that all who joined him and took up arms would tri-

16. Marabouts were Islamic holy men, often scholars of the Koran. They dispensed more than just Koranic wisdom, however, for they also provided magic amulets for various purposes, foretold the future, and were thought (especially by Christians) to be able to cast spells. The "famous sorcerer of the city" mentioned by Dan in note 4 above, who was credited with foiling Charles V's invasion of Algiers, was one such marabout.

umph, for the muskets of their enemies would fail to fire, while their own would shoot unerringly. Having convinced them with these reasons, and others like them, this marabout assembled a powerful army of Moors and Arabs to assault the town's Algerian garrison.

The Algerians, receiving news of this rebellion, assembled a force of janissaries and paid soldiers, of which there is always a large number in their city, well-armed and in good order, and rushed to confront the rebels. Though the Algerian forces numbered little more than eleven or twelve hundred against ten thousand, they nevertheless discharged their muskets with such effect that they immediately put the rebels to flight. They then pursued the rebels and cut them to pieces, taking many prisoners, including the marabout himself, and thirty-two of his main followers. They immediately flayed the prisoners alive and then returned to Algiers, victorious, parading through the streets displaying on pikes the skins of the defeated rebels to celebrate their triumph.

All this happened in 1627.

Once again, Jón Jónsson's description of events does not quite match Father Dan's. Jón's depiction is also a bit confused. He writes: "the sons of the renegades, who here are called kardooleis, have wanted to take over the town from the Turks and make it their own, and the Turks' masters make war secretly against the Tremesen, who belong to this king's town, so the Turks and they were fighting over possession of the town. Because of this, the Turks became so cautious that they walked with unsheathed daggers and swords under their coats into their churches." Jón seems to be conflating the two different rebellions here. It is also not clear who, exactly, the "Turks' masters" might be or why they would be "secretly" confronting the revolt of a subject city.

It is not, perhaps, surprising that Jón might be a little unclear about events. Remember how he concluded his letter: "Written in a great haste, during the night when all slept." He likely had little time for elaborate descriptions or careful revision. More than this, though, as a slave, he would have led a constrained life, and so would have to rely on hearsay and gossip for the details of events unfolding around him. A man like Father Dan, on the other hand, would have had far more freedom both to go where he wanted and to talk with whom he wanted, and as a member of the Trinitarians, a ransoming order, he would have had direct contacts with members of the Divan. All this makes Father Dan a more reliable source than Jón.

Jón's description also suffers from another drawback: not only does he not seem terribly conversant with events, he does not really appear to be all that interested in the details. He introduces his description of the rebellions with the following: "Since the big punishment began to be meted out on the wicked inhabitants of these towns for their villainy, they have rioted among themselves." To him (not surprisingly, perhaps), all the inhabitants of Algiers are essentially the same—"wicked"—and his intent seems to be to illustrate how those inhabitants are blighted by their own wickedness rather than to faithfully record actual events in detail.

His observation that "there are few Turks left behind here" and that "the king of Spain has a ship prepared and sixty galleys … waiting to sail" appears to indicate that he expected the Spanish to seize the opportunity and attack Algiers. No such liberating attack ever happened, and it seems this is Jón indulging in the sort of classic wish-fulfillment fantasy all such captives surely needed to nurture as a counterbalance to the bitter thought of lifelong servitude.

---

As well as details about current events in Algiers, Jón's letter also present us with the following—most intriguing—pair of sentences: *No so fullan para los bastimentos, sino lavansensia de los demas amigos mios. A foderoso sonnar Dios remidiet sus probetis Psclavos.*

The editor of the standard Icelandic language edition (1969) of *The Travels* says this about these sentences: "It is not possible to make any sense of the words, and they are probably the result of mistakes by the copyists." It is certainly difficult to decipher these two sentences. The first appears to be partly Spanish (e.g., *para los bastimentos,* "for the supplies"; *amigos mios,* "my friends"), the second possibly part Latin (e.g., *probetis,* perhaps the second-person plural present active subjunctive of *probō,* to approve, to test; then again, *probetis* could possibly be a Latinate ending of "probado," Spanish for "proven" or "tested").

Neither the sentences nor the combination of languages make simple straightforward sense, though. There are also what appear to be errors on the part of the copyist(s): "foderoso" is likely *poderoso* ("powerful" in Spanish), and "Psclavos" almost certainly should be *esclavos* ("slave" in Spanish). The text here is taken verbatim from a handwritten copy of the original letter (such copies were frequently sent to bishops and other influential people). The original letter disappeared long ago. Icelandic copyists often had little or no knowledge of Latin, and were highly unlikely to have any knowledge at all of languages such as Spanish.

There are, however, other elements to this. There were many Spanish slaves in Algiers when Jón was there, and he might have picked up a Spanish expression somehow and written it down in some fashion that eventually became garbled. But Jón was an educated, literate man, and perfectly capable of writing good Latin, as his letter shows, and most likely capable of writing down clear Spanish if he wanted to, even if it was just a phrase he had learned by rote. There is always the possibility that there might be some Lingua Franca thrown in here. Lingua Franca— also called Sabir, from the verb "to know"—was the common language spoken by the variegated groups in the Maghreb. It was a mix of Italian, Spanish, Portuguese, French, Greek, Turkish, Arabic, and Berber. The particular blend of languages varied depended on the location, with Spanish being an especially prominent European component in Algiers. Not a great deal is known about the structure of Lingua Franca (it was a spoken, not a written language), but it seems clear it had a stripped-down grammar. Verbs ended (mostly) either in *-ir* or *-ar*. Nouns were not declined and generally did not form plurals.[17]

In the sentences from Jón's letter, we have "sonar" in the second sentence, which could conceivably be a Lingua Franca verb. But it does not make any clear sense as a verb, and since Lingua Franca nouns did not typically form plurals, the "amigos mios" seems to disqualify these sentences as being Lingua Franca in any simple way. All in all, then, these sentences present a puzzle. We can guess at the meaning, though.

Here is a possible translation: "I have no money for material things, only the support of my remaining friends. The treatment of almighty God tests his slaves."

This is based on the following loose interpretation: I have no [*No so*, Italian: "I do not know"] money [*fullan*, Turkish: "money"] for material things [*para los bastimentos*, Spanish: "for supplies"], only [*sinon*, Spanish: "but"] the support [*lavansensia*, "support," a pure guess] of my remaining friends [*de los demas amigos mios*, Spanish: "of my remaining friends"]. The treatment [*remidiet*, "remedy," and so "treatment," a guess] of almighty [*poderoso* for *foderoso*, Spanish: "powerful"] God [*Dios*, Spanish: "God"] tests [*probetis*, Latin: "test"] his slaves [*esclavos* for *Psclavos*, *sus esclavos*, Spanish: "his slaves"].

---

17. For those who might be interested, Molière's *Le Bourgeois Gentilhomme* contains a short (literary) example of Lingua Franca: "Se ti sabir, / Ti respondir; / Se non sabir, / Tazir, tazir." [If you know, / You will reply; / If you do not know, / Be silent, be silent.]

The second sentence might also be rendered as follows: "For the almighty Lord God aids his tested slaves."

This is based on the following: For the almighty Lord God [*señor* for *sonar*; *a poderoso señor Dios*, Spanish: "for the almighty Lord God"] aids [*remedia*, Spanish: "aids"] his tested slaves [*sus probetis esclavos*, Spanish: "his tested slaves"].

Much of the above is, of course, pure guesswork, but given the context, these sentences must surely be expressing something along these lines. The more interesting question, perhaps, is what prompted Jón to include these sentences in his letter in the first place. He was an educated man. His erudition is clearly displayed in his letter.[18] One presumes he expected his readers (his parents, the bishop, the school master, the teachers of the Skálholt Latin School he mentions in the letter) to be able to make sense of whatever it was he originally wrote. Unfortunately, his intentions (like the clear meaning of the two sentences) are now lost to us.

---

Jón Jónsson is known in Icelandic history as Jón Jónsson the Scholar (to distinguish him from innumerable other Jón Jónssons). In his case, "scholar" meant graduate from one of the Latin Schools, either at Skálholt or in Hólar, in North Iceland, institutions intended to educate pastors. Jón was from a well-to-do, influential family. He had only recently returned to Járngerðarstaðir farm, the family farm in Grindavík, as a newly minted graduate, presumably to take up a position of authority there, either with the church or the local administration, when he was taken captive (a dramatic example of being in the wrong place at the wrong time).

18. The wealth of Latinate religious allusion in Jón's letter can be explained, in part, by his education, but he also might have meant to reassure his readers that he was still a dedicated Christian and had not "turned" (i.e., had not renounced his religion and converted to Islam).

He was captured along with his mother, Guðrún Jónsdóttir, his brothers, Helgi Jónsson and Héðinn Jónsson, and his uncles, Halldór Jónsson and Jón Jónsson (his mother's brothers). His mother and his uncle Halldór, who were sold into slavery in Salé, in Morocco, were ransomed by a Dutchman and returned to Iceland in 1628. Héðinn, Jón's brother in Salé, eventually gained his freedom but never returned to Iceland. Helgi, Jón's other brother, who was with him in Algiers, was among the twenty-seven Icelanders whose ransom was paid and who eventually returned home in 1637. There is no record of what happened to Jón's uncle Jón, who worked "as a ploughman for a merchant" in Salé.

As a young, well-educated man of means, Jón would have been a leading figure among the captive Icelanders—and undoubtedly a highly prized commodity among his captors. There is a story that during the ransom negotiations in 1636, the asking price for one of the captive Icelanders was so high that negotiations broke down. That too-highly priced slave was quite possibly Jón Jónsson.

Jón wrote another letter, in 1633, which was used by Björn Jónsson as one of the sources for the *Tyrkjaráns-saga* (*The Turkish Raid Saga*). That letter, however, is now lost to us. The letter translated here took four years to reach Iceland.

There is no clear documentation on what fate eventually befell Jón Jónsson.

## Anonymous Letter

August 21, 1635—Algiers

A letter from the captives in Algiers about their circumstances, their redemption, the betrayal of those sent to redeem them, and the untrustworthiness of letters from Iceland.

Letter and supplication from the Icelandic captives in the Turkish Barbari to the lords in Copenhagen, Anno 1635.

TO OUR MOST honest lords and masters, spiritual and worldly, in the royal town of Copenhagen, to our loyal lords, yes, to all those who love Jesus and take care of their brethren, this letter is humbly written from Algiers in 1635.

God-fearing lords, friends, and brothers in God.

May God the father, the son, and the holy spirit maintain in freedom and liberty, fortune and blessing, long life and good health, all who see, hear, and read this letter, and may you have compassion for those poor souls in captivity. God preserve you, body and soul, from all evil. In Jesus Christ. Amen.

We, the followers of Jesus Christ, witnesses to his wounds, have been led away into captivity and have ourselves been wounded and martyred, but we bear the seal of the Lord God on our foreheads, and we live in hope of the mercy that was pledged by the innocent blood of the lamb [Jesus Christ] who dwells in Heaven and who will, on Judgement Day, reward each and every man as his acts deserve, bringing that which was done in secret out into the light before the holy angels and the elect.

In His name, and in the name of those souls who have passed away and dwell before the throne of God, we cry out for retribution upon those who have bound us in chains and keep us imprisoned, who daily distress our hearts and wound our bodies, who torture and constrain our souls—and upon all who support this. May God forgive those, if they be worthy, who have hindered our redemption from the power of these blasphemers and persecutors. They who have come here must, for their own souls' sake, answer for the deaths of young children, for the apostasy of those who have deserted the faith, for the afflictions of the living, wounded in soul and body, and for the torment and gnashing of teeth caused by our long captivity.[1] The Lord who sits in judgment over the terrestrial globe, the moon, the sun, and all the stars in the firmament is witness to the sluggishness of the hearts of men, to their unscrupulousness, to the dwindling of charity, to the contempt men have for their poor brethren, and to their obliviousness of the last day of judgment. Those dissemblers, those brothers of Nabal,[2] companions of Judas, those Architophels.[3] The blood of Abel is not yet cold, even though it was shed hundreds of years ago. It still reveals itself in bloody-handed violence and heartfelt tears sent up to heaven. Is there now no mercy, no charity, no awakened

1. The writer is referring here to two representatives of the Danish Crown whom he discusses further on in the letter. These men arrived in Algiers, separately, to redeem the Icelandic captives, but each used the ransom money to enrich himself instead. The writer's accusation seems to be that these two men bore a moral responsibility for the consequences of their actions, for as a result of their not redeeming the captives, children had died, people had "turned Turk," and the captive Icelanders, who had continued to be mistreated ("wounded in soul and body"), had fallen deeper into despair. It should be remembered that, at the time this letter was written, the Icelandic captives were entering their ninth year of slavery.

2. Nabal, of the house of Caleb, was "churlish and evil in his doings." 1 Samuel, 25, relates the story of how David sent ten young men to Nabal with a message of peace, and how Nabal spurned them.

3. "Achitophel" is a variant of "Ahitophel," the Gilonite who counseled Absalom to revolt against his father, David, in 2 Samuel 13–19.

149

conscience? Are there no God-fearing men? Do we have no merciful king? Are we without righteous masters and defenders? Without God-fearing preachers? Without parents, friends and brothers, that they do not feel in their hearts our mortal distress and anguish? A blood-stained rod hangs over us, so that we suffer in despair and darkness in the power of the Turks, those destroyers, fettered by heavy chains in the dungeons of those false demons, as were those under the Pharoahs, while the captains' flags[4] and the standard of that seven-crowned dragon Mahomet[5] [Muhammad] fly over our heads.

God knows that it is a pain as sharp as a double-edged sword, and more bitter than death, yes, more hurtful than bloody injuries to know that those who have been here twice to Algiers with our ransom money have used it instead for trade, to make profit for themselves, and have stolen our liberty, for

4. It is not clear who or what the "captains' flags" might represent. In chapter IV of *A True and Faithful Account of the Religion and Manners of the Mohammetans ... with an Account of the Author's Being Taken Captive*, Joseph Pitts describes the Algerian janissary military garrison on the march: "They move but two in a breast each rank keeping at a considerable distance so that a thousand men make a great shew [sic], and a very long train. The *Cayah-Beulick*, or Lieutenant, rides in the van of the army with two *Hoages*, or Clerks, each of them bearing a flag." It is possible the writer of the letter witnessed marches of this sort, and that the "captains' flags" refer to these janissary military flags. Pitts also writes, in chapter VI: "The second time of their [prayer] services is ... about two of the clock in the afternoon, which they call *Eulea Nomas*; at which time they hoist up a white flag on a pole on the top of the steeple [i.e., the minaret of the mosque] ... to give notice to people that they be in due preparation [for prayer]." It is possible the writer of the letter saw these minaret flags on a daily basis. Such flags, whether in the hands of janissaries or flying from a minaret, would have been powerful emblems of the repression under which the Icelandic captives suffered. See Auchterlonie (*Encountering Islam*) or Vitkus (*Piracy, Slavery, and Redemption*) in the Suggestions for Further Reading section; both works contain versions of Pitts's captivity narrative.

5. The writer of the letter is likely alluding here to the seven-headed beast described by John in Revelation 13:1: "And I stood upon the sand of the sea, and saw a beast rise up out of the sea, having seven heads and ten horns, and upon his horns ten crowns, and upon his heads the name of blasphemy." The writer's accusation seems to be that "Mahomet" is (or represents, or is represented by) the beast.

they never admitted that they could free anyone, or even that they were here to do so. Instead, they told us to petition our gracious master the king, in the name of God, for our freedom, and then they filled simpleminded, poor fellows with fair words and went on their way, one with hides, another with chests of sugar, leaving behind them only the smoke of their lying words.[6] They were here under our praiseworthy king's name, but they left us only God's name to call upon, He who preserves us and whom we keep in our hearts through difficulties and disappointment. We can only trust in the living God's forgiveness and pray for our excellent lord the king's mercy, and that by his *real claridad Neombransa mobil*[7] after his coronation oath, and for justice in the name of God, he will graciously remember us and deal with those who work against our freedom and force us to accept *pour facesa*[8] our exile as if we were

6. There is no documentation for who these two men might have been. It is possible that they were representatives of wealthy Danes or Icelanders sent to ransom only a select few of the Icelandic captives. This might explain why they told the captives to "petition our gracious master the king, in the name of God, for [your] freedom." Whatever the actual details of the situation might have been, the writer of the letter clearly believed that these men used ransom money to enrich themselves, at the captives' expense, by buying hides and chests of sugar to sell at a profit—and so reneged on their moral responsibilities.

7. This is the phrase in the Icelandic text of the letter. Like other such tantalizing phrases, this one seems to be part Spanish. If "claridad" is a copyist's mistaken rendering of "caridad" (charity), then "real claridad" could mean "royal charity," which would make sense in this context. The meaning of "Neombransa mobil" is uncertain.

8. This is the phrase in the Icelandic text of the letter. Given the learned tone of this letter, one is tempted to interpret these words as an inept copyist's corruption of some standard Latin phrase: something like *per fas et nefas* ("through right or wrong"), for example, might be a possible candidate, meaning, conceivably, that the captives had been abandoned to survive their ordeal by fair means or foul. This is a bit of a stretch, though. There does not appear to be any standard Latin phrase close enough in form to "pour facesa" to be an obvious choice, and it remains unclear exactly what it means here—or even what language the phrase might have originally been written in.

the sons of Rubens [Reuben] in the land of Gilead,[9] so that we would lose our inheritance in Canaan. They are keepers of the dusk[10] and like the seven sleepers of winter,[11] and they believe, perhaps, with Catullo Lesbiano: *noctem esse pepetuam unam dormiendam,*[12] and that they never have to answer for their deeds if they know well how to steal, so long as the crime is not found out or looked into. It is obvious that those two men have cheated us. Now there is the third one left. Nobody

9. Reuben (also Re'uven) was the firstborn of Jacob and Leah but forfeited his birthright after lying with his father's concubine. The sons of Reuben (along with the Gadites and half the tribe of Manasseh) were vanquished by the Assyrians and exiled, becoming one of the lost tribes of Israel (1 Chronicles 5).

10. It is unclear what this phrase refers to.

11. The writer is perhaps referring here to some form of the hagiographic tale found in Jacobus (Jacques) de Voragine's *Legenda Aurea* [*Golden Legends*] (circa 1260) about seven Christians who, with God's help, escaped persecution by sleeping for 360 (or 180, depending on the version) years in a cave. It is not altogether clear, but the writer of the letter seems to be saying that the men who cheated the captives believed that they could avoid the just consequences of their evil deeds by letting "sleeping dogs lie," so to speak.

12. "Catullo" here refers to the classical Latin poet Gaius Valerius Catullus. "Lesbiano" refers to the poem known as Catullus 5, or Carmen 5, which is an ode to "Lesbia"—the pseudonym Catullus used for his real-life lover. The actual line (slightly misquoted, or miscopied, in this letter) appears in the poem as follows: *soles occidere et redire possunt: / nobis cum semel occidit brevis lux, / nox est perpetua una dormienda* (Suns can rise and set. / But for us, when our brief light sets / There is one perpetual night's sleep). Thomas Campion (English poet, physician, and musician) in 1601 wrote a loose poetic translation of Carmen 5 that conveys the sense of the poem very clearly. Here is the first stanza:

> My sweetest Lesbia, let us live and love,
> And, though the sager sort our deeds reprove,
> Let us not weigh them: heaven's great lamps do dive
> Into their west, and straight again revive,
> But, soon as once set is our little light,
> Then must we sleep one ever-during night.

The writer of the letter seems to be quoting Catullus's pagan *carpe diem* sentiment as an example of erroneous thinking. Christians, after all, do not go into "perpetual night" when they die: they go before the Lord, where they receive judgment and are rewarded or punished for all eternity.

knows what he will do.[13] The Moors and the Spanish say that the *Paracletos* is Mahometh [Muhammad].[14] But what means then our freedom, given by our God and the lord our king and his subordinates, if they who have been here in Algiers engaged in trade, using our ransom money, have left us poor slaves still prisoners? We can only hold on here and say with the Spanish Cardinal Eldinore: *dios toth poaerso del mundo y vesos pues mas sus et cælo.*[15]

We also wish to say that all the letters which are written and sent yearly from here, and often written again, and sent again, seem never to have been received, except only the letters which went with that God-fearing Master Peter Christianson, K. and M. Antonio, and Possedore de Laskinses, because these men were faithful. We have survived here for eight and a half

13. This third man was Paul de Willum (also de Willumis), who worked for the Danish authorities (he is mentioned in a letter from the king of Denmark, Christian IV, in 1634, as "our messenger in Amsterdam"). De Willum had official orders to buy out as many Icelandic captives as possible. Working through merchant networks in Amsterdam and Marseilles, he eventually redeemed a total of 35 Icelanders.

14. "Paracletos" is a variant of "Paraclete," from the Greek, meaning "advocate or helper." John 14, 26: "But the Paraclete, the Holy Ghost, whom the Father will send in my name, he will teach you all things and bring all things to your mind, whatsoever I shall have said to you." The writer of the letter seems to be saying that Muslims in Algiers claimed Muhammad was God's Paraclete. How this connects with the sentence that follows it is not altogether clear.

15. This is the phrase in the Icelandic text of the letter. As with other similar phrases, this one appears to be Spanish corrupted by copyists' errors. The Spanish phrase (mostly misspelled by modern conventions) "dios toth poaerso del mundo" translates fairly straightforwardly as "God all powerful over the earth." The phrase "y vesos pues mas sus" is more problematic. "Pues mas" translates as "and more" or "in addition to." There is no obvious noun or verb in this phrase, however, unless "vesos" is a misconjugation of the Spanish verb "ver," meaning "to see." But even if that is so, it does not help establish any clear meaning. "Et cælo" can obviously mean "and Heaven." A reasonable, though not entirely literal, translation might read something like this: "God has power over the Earth and also in Heaven." We have assumed that "Eldinore" is a name rather than a corruption of some Spanish word. It is unclear who "Cardinal Eldinore" might have been.

years without even one little letter from our beloved homeland, without knowledge or certainty of our friends, our dear brothers and fellows, and nothing at all regarding our redemption other than what newly arrived people tell us, that taxes and customs duties have been given yearly in the name of God in all our merciful lord the king's majestic kingdom for the poor prisoners here in Algiers and other places in Africa. We know the fault lies not with those who have written letters to us but, rather, with those who convey those same letters. Even if the merchants come so far as Legornam [Livorno], the letters seem to go no further than into the sea by the fishing port, so that we piteous captives get nothing with which we can revitalize our spirits or arrange our freedom. They scorn us and believe captives such as we to be unworthy dogs, not deserving of even one small piece of grace given from their position of freedom and liberty, and so we get no letters of comfort from our heartfelt friends, brothers, or beloved homeland, because all these merchants act the same.

You are many times blessed by God, you who have kept your bodily freedom and mental liberty, dwelling in God's blessed word and his sacrament, but we are always miserable and downtrodden, longing for what we have lost. May God maintain you in your freedom, and may He grant us that freedom, too, we who once knew how sweet and graceful God had been to us but who are now punished, so that we should fear, love, and know Him. As David said: *dixit: bonum est mihi Domine etc. Regnum lucis via crucis* [He said: It is good for me, Lord, etc. The kingdom of light by the way of the Cross]. We poor wretched Christian prisoners, your exiled brothers, beg you, for God's sake, and for the sake of charity, to show sympathy for our grief, to let our suffering reach into your hearts so that you feel pity for our dreadful struggle. We must eat our bread of sorrow with flowing tears, and live in hope that, in the name of God, we will be delivered from the hands of the ill-willed before we are undone by death. We wish that you will pray for us, in all congregations, by all God's holy altars and pulpits, in all our merciful lord the king's majestic kingdom, that compassionate God will aid us in gaining our freedom and bring us to a Christian country. In the name of Jesus Christ, and for Jesus Christ, Amen.

We beseech you all, whom Jesus has commanded to love and aid your brothers, you who wish to help and put God's words into actions and do His will, to remember and aid us poor captives. May the power of God, which is beyond all understanding, take care of your hearts, and may you dwell with Jesus Christ for all eternity. Amen.

Our good lords, we kneel before you, we wretched poor Icelanders, captive in Algiers.

---

Written in Algiers, in the Barbari, on 21 August, Anno 1635.

There is no clear documentation for who wrote this letter. Indications are, however, that the author was Jón Jónsson (the same Jón Jónsson as wrote the previous letter). Being an educated man from a well-to-do family, Jón would have been an obvious candidate to serve as spokesperson for the Icelandic captives. The letter also shows some of the same elements of his previous letter: the learned interweaving of biblical references, the use of Latin, and, more distinctively perhaps, the use of Spanish (apparently corrupted by copyists' errors). Jón seems to have been a remarkable man, intelligent, well-educated, with an extensive knowledge not only of Scripture but also, if this letter is any indication, of Latin classical pagan writings as well.

Jón's use of Spanish seems to indicate that he had some interactions with Spanish speakers. During this time, there were many Spanish slaves in Algiers, and Spain had one of the best organized systems for ransoming captives. Jón could well have met not only Spanish slaves but also Spanish clergy involved in the redemption process. (It is even conceivable that he might have met the Frenchman Pierre Dan, the Trinitarian friar who was in Algiers in 1634 and who wrote the *Histoire de Barbarie*.) Jón would have been able to communicate with such men in Latin. The fact that as a Protestant (Lutheran), he quotes a Spanish (Catholic) cardinal in this letter would seem to be evidence for something along these lines. Learned men held captive in Algiers formed a kind of society of their own, for their shared education meant they had more in common with each other than with other slaves.[16] Whether or not—and to what extent—this society crossed religious or cultural boundaries is harder to know. It is interesting to speculate on where, exactly, Jón might have learned his Spanish (he had to have picked it up from somewhere, after all), and on whether a Protestant such as he was actually able to overcome the barriers of religion and culture to converse with Catholic clergy. We shall never know.

This letter was particularly difficult to translate, and we had to resort to conveying the sense of the text rather than the "letter"—more here than with any other part of this book. A couple of reasons—aside from copyists' errors—might explain why the text of the letter is so difficult to make clear sense of. First, there is some indication that the letter might not have originally been written in Icelandic at all, but, rather, in Latin, and then

16. We know from other sources, for instance, that when Miguel de Cervantes, author of *Don Quixote*, was enslaved in Algiers, he wrote poetry and discussed it at length with Antonio de Sosa, the erudite Portuguese cleric who wrote the *Topographia, e historia general de Argel* (*Topography and General History of Algiers*).

translated into Icelandic at a later date—and been confused in the translation. A Latin text of the letter exists in the *Historia Ecclesiastica Islandæ* (*Ecclesiastical History of Iceland*). Unfortunately, it is hardly any clearer than the Icelandic version. Second, the letter is written by somebody who is obviously in the grip of intense moral outrage at the way he and his fellow captives have been maltreated. One can imagine Jón crouched in a secret corner somewhere, scribbling furiously by candlelight ("Those dissemblers! Those brothers of Nabal! Companions of Judas! Those Architophels!"), venting his indignation and balked anger. There would have been no easy opportunity for him to revise such a letter, and the incoherence may very well stem from some version of this situation.

Though the details of the text were hard to sort out, the letter's general tone of outrage comes through with unequivocal clarity. The writer had good reason for such anger, given the circumstances he outlines. There is no clear documentation to support his accusation that on two separate occasions, men who had been sent to Algiers in the name of the Danish crown to ransom the Icelandic captives used the ransom funds to enrich themselves. It is not too difficult to believe, though. Such misuse of funds must have been lamentably common. Imagine seeing your redeemer finally arrive (the person who will organize the liberation you have spent years yearning for, praying fervently for) and then finding out that he has betrayed his trust—and having this occur not once but twice. It must have been devastating.

This letter, perhaps more than any of the others, dramatizes the utter powerlessness captives in Algeria must have felt. In the course of their daily existence as slaves, raising sufficient funds to ransom themselves was an impossibly difficult task. Without family resources or connections in high places—and without the sorts of redemptive societies such as the Trinitarians or Mercedarians that Catholic captives could rely on—the Icelanders were completely at the mercy of their sovereign (and of their sovereign's representatives). Their only recourse was to plead for ransom, or, as in the case of this letter, rail against the injustice of it all and try to persuade—or shame—the authorities into doing something.

The Danish authorities did respond, but it took the better part of a decade. The first agreement to buy out a captive was negotiated in August 1635 (the very month this letter was written),[17] but the process was not finally completed until the middle of the next year. In the end, of the nearly 400 Icelanders originally taken captive in the raid of 1627, only 35 were redeemed in the 1635/36 ransoming process. Some Icelandic captives had already been redeemed privately before this date, but the number amounted to only a handful. None of the captives in Salé appears to have been ransomed during the 1635/36 negotiations. By this time, though, some of them were resident in Algiers and show up on the list of those redeemed. The ransom demanded by some slaves' owners was too high and negotiations failed. There was, after all, a finite amount of ransom money available, and it had to be stretched as far as possible. We suspect this happened to Jón Jónsson himself, and that he ended his days unhappily as a slave in Algiers.

17. One cannot help but wonder why Jón Jónsson (if he was indeed the author of this letter) is ignorant of the ransom negotiations that have already begun as he is writing. As with other aspects of this and the other letters, however, we will likely never know the answer.

# Appendixes ᑰ

WE HAVE INCLUDED four sections here for readers who
wish to explore in greater detail the context of the Tyrkjaránið.
The first section, Algiers and Salé, contains information about
the cities of Algiers and Salé in the seventeenth century. The
second section, The Icelandic Background, contains general information about Iceland in the seventeenth century, as well as
details about the Westman Islands and Reverend Ólafur himself, plus some discussion of units of measurement and currencies. The third section, The Manuscript Sources, discusses the
various manuscripts we referred to in translating *The Travels*
and the accompanying letters. The fourth section, The Times,
is a general discussion of the early modern European context of
*The Travels* and of Reverend Ólafur himself.

# Algiers and Salé

We feel it would be useful for the reader to have a clearer sense of what the city of Algiers was like when Revered Ólafur and the other Icelanders arrived there. And since the captives from Grindavík were taken to Salé (Salé is mentioned in the letters), we have included a brief section on that city as well.

## Algiers

After the Reconquista culminated in the expulsion of the Muslim population from Granada in 1492, the Spanish expanded into North Africa. By the beginning of the second decade of the sixteenth century, Spanish forces had occupied a number of Maghrebi cities (Oran, Mers-el-Kébir, Borgie, Tripoli) and forced others to sign treaties of capitulation. Algiers was among these latter. In 1510, the city signed a treaty acknowledging Spanish sovereignty and committed to paying an annual tribute. To enforce this arrangement, the Spanish built an offshore fort (El Peñón de Argel) on one of the islands in the bay on which Algiers sat and mounted cannons there to dominate the city.

In 1516 (the year King Ferdinand II of Spain died), the rulers of Algiers sought help to escape Spanish domination. They called upon two brothers, famous for their victories against the Spanish: Aruj and Khizr—better known as the Barbarossa brothers. Instead of aiding Algiers, however, Aruj, the elder brother, mounted a coup and took control of the city. Unable to defeat the Spanish unaided, Khizr offered allegiance to the Ottoman Porte (Aruj had been killed by then) and was given the title of *Beylerbey* (from the Turkish, meaning bey of beys— commander of commanders), and an Ottoman military contingent was sent to the city. After a series of bloody conflicts, Khizr and his forces finally ousted the Spanish from the Peñon in 1529, and Algiers began its ascendency as the corsair capital of the Maghreb.

The city itself is located on the western shore of a bay on what is now the Algerian Mediterranean coast and faces roughly northeast. It was built on a mountain slope rising up from the sea, so its buildings ascended the slope. In Reverend Ólafur's time, the city was divided into two sections: a lower portion (known as Al-Wata—the Plains), containing the public buildings and the commercial, administrative, and military sectors, and an upper portion (known as Al-Gabal—the Mountain), containing private dwellings, tightly packed with individual houses and neighborhoods. At the top of Al-Gabal sat the Kasbah (Al-Qasaba—the Fort), some 400 feet (122 meters) above sea level and enclosed by its own walls. These three sections together formed a single municipal entity, bounded by an encircling, defensive wall studded with towers. A series of gates set into the wall gave access to and from the city. Roads from the five main gates converged in the center of Al-Wata.

Perhaps the best way to get a sense of what all this looked like is to start with contemporary accounts of it. The details below are excerpted from four works: *Topographia, e historia general de Argel* (*Topography and General History of Algiers*);[1] *Relation*

1. The details of Algiers are excerpted from chapters 5, 6, 7, 8, 10, and 39 of *An Early Modern Dialogue with Islam: Antonio de Sosa's Topography of Algiers*, edited and translated by Maria Antonia Garcés and Dianna De Armas. The *Topographia* was originally published in Spanish, in 1612 (a quarter of a century after de Sosa's death), under the name of Fray Diego de Haedo. The reasons why it did not bear

*de la captivité du sieur Emanuel d'Aranda mené esclave à Alger en l'an 1640 et mise en liberté l'an 1642 (Story of the Captivity of Emanuel d' Aranda, Enslaved in Algiers in 1640 and liberated in 1642);*[2] *Memorável Relação da Perda da Nau Conceição (A Memorable Account of the Loss of the Ship Conceição);*[3] *and Histoire de Barbarie et de ses corsairs, des royaumes, et des villes d'Alger, de Tunis, de Salé, et de Tripoli (History of the Barbary and its corsairs, its kingdoms, and the cities of Algiers, Tunis, and Tripoli).*[4]

The *Topographia*, published in 1612, was written by Antonio de Sosa, who was enslaved in Algiers from 1577 to 1581 (the *Topographia* was published posthumously). The *Relation*, published in 1656, was written by Emanuel d'Aranda, who was enslaved in Algiers from 1640 to 1641. The *Relação* was written in 1627 by João Mascarenhas, who was enslaved in Algiers from 1621 to 1626. The *Histoire de Barbarie* was first published in 1637 by Father Pierre Dan, a Trinitarian[5] friar who was in Algiers in 1634. De Sosa predates Reverend Ólafur by nearly fifty years,

---

de Sosa's own name are too complicated to go into here. The Introduction to *An Early Modern Dialogue with Islam* makes everything clear. See the Suggestions for Further Reading section for bibliographical details for this and the other three primary sources used in this section.

2. The details of Algiers are excerpted from the fourth "Relation" (titled "Of the Scituation, [sic] Strength, and Government of the City of Algiers") in *The history of Algiers and its slavery with many remarkable particularities of Africk, written by the Sieur Emanuel d' Aranda, sometime a slave there, English'd by John Davies* (published in 1666). We have modernized spelling, capitalization, and so on.

3. The details of Algiers are excerpted from part 2, chapters 1, 4, 7, and 8 of *Esclave à Alger: récit de captivité de João Mascarenhas (Enslaved in Algiers: the story of the captivity of João Mascarenhas)*, translated from the original Portuguese by Paul Teyssier. The translation from the French is our own.

4. The details of Algiers are excerpted from book 2, chapter 2, and book 5, chapters 2, 5, 6, and 7 of *Histoire de Barbarie et de ses corsairs, des royaumes, et des villes d'Alger, de Tunis, de Salé, et de Tripoli.* The translation from the French is our own.

5. The Trinitarians (the Order of the Most Holy Trinity) and the Mercedarians (Our Lady of Mercy) were the two main Catholic Redemptionist orders, dedicated to ransoming enslaved (Catholic) Christians.

and d'Aranda follows him in Algiers by a little over a decade, but both Mascarenhas and Dan were in Algiers within a few years of Reverend Ólafur. These four sources, between them, provide us with a detailed on-the-spot account of what Algiers was like in Reverend Ólafur's day.

Here is de Sosa on the physical layout of the city:

Algiers, including its entire circumference and ramparts, may be envisioned in the image of a crossbow, including the string. The arch that encircles the city measures some 1,800 paces, and that of the string that extends over the seascape some 1,600 paces, so that the total circumference adds up to 3,400 paces. The height of these ancient ramparts is some thirty spans. The thickness of the ramparts is some eleven or twelve spans. Beyond this wall that encircles the city on all sides, Barbarossa constructed, in 1532, another stretch of wall, closing the distance between the city and the island in order to make the port. With a length of some three hundred paces, a width of more than ten spans, and a height of some fifteen.

Here is d'Aranda:

It [Algiers] is in a manner square, and about three thousand paces in compass. The Walls are of brick built after the ancient way of fortification, with little square Towers. About three hundred paces from the City, there is, in the Sea, a little Island, which in the year 1530 was joined to the city by a mole, made for the safety of ships and galleys.

Mascarenhas echoes de Sosa: "The circumference of the city is 1,800 paces on the landward side, and 1,600 paces along the shoreward side. That is to say, 3,400 paces in total."[6]

A "pace" as a unit of measurement is normally considered

6. One should perhaps be a little suspicious of the exact match between Mascarenhas' and de Sosa's measurements of the city. Mascarenhas was clearly familiar with de Sosa's book (it had been first published 15 years before he wrote his), and there are portions of his description of Algiers in the *Relação* that read as if he cribbed them directly from de Sosa's work.

to be about 30 inches (76 centimeters), so 3,400 paces is about 8,500 feet (2,590 meters), or a little over a mile and a half. Three thousand paces is about 7,500 feet (2,286 meters), a little under a mile and a half. Splitting the difference makes the city's circumference about a mile and a half (2.4 kilometers). De Sosa and Mascarenhas agree that the distance across the "string" of de Sosa's imaginary crossbow (i.e., the straight-line distance across the harbor) was 1,600 paces, which is 4,000 feet (1,219 meters), or a little over three quarters of a mile (1.2 kilometers).][7]

In more familiar terms, one can imagine Algiers, seen from above, as being shaped like a capital letter *D*. (Observers at the time said the city narrowed as it ascended, so to be a more accurate representation, the apex of the half-circle of the *D* would have to be squished.) The letter's vertical upright represents the harbor front, about three quarters of a mile long (1.2 kilometers), and the half-circle curve represents the perimeter of the city, about a mile and a half around (2.4 kilometers). Some modern estimates of the size of the seventeenth century city are a little larger (10,170 feet / 3,100 meters for the total length of the walls, for instance), but even if one assumes de Sosa, d'Aranda, and Mascarenhas all underestimated the overall size to some extent, it is clear that, by modern standards, seventeenth century Algiers was not especially large.

Since the city was built on a slope rising up from the coast, its buildings ascended progressively higher, tier upon tier. Here is d'Aranda's description: "The situation of this famous den of pirates is on the ascent of a mountain, which rises by degrees

7. We can do a quick "ballpark" check on these figures. Assuming the shape of Algiers to be a half circle, we can apply the standard $C = \pi d$ formula (circumference equals pi times diameter) and plug in the numbers. Using 1,600 paces as the diameter, we get a circumference of 5,026 paces for the full circle. Half of that is 2,513 paces, close enough to d'Aranda's and de Sosa's measurements (3,000–3,400 paces) to make sense, since the city would not, of course, have been a perfect half-circle.

from the seaside up into the country, representing to those who sail by it the several stories [i.e., tiers of seats] of a theatre." Here is Dan: "This city, with its whitewashed houses, looks extremely nice when you approach it from the sea. It presents itself to one's view ... mounting like an amphitheater. Even though it is square, the city seems much less wide at the top than at the bottom, which happens, according to the rules of perspective ... and it seems to form a pyramidal shape."

With its whitewashed buildings, seen rising up out of the shoreline from the sea on a sunny day, the city could present a splendid appearance—if those viewing it were in a state of mind to appreciate such a sight.

The Arabic name for Algiers is Al-Jazāʾir (the Islands), taken from the several islands that once dotted the bay, on one of which the Spanish built their offshore fort (El Peñon) in 1510. In Reverend Ólafur's day, these islands were merged into a single entity connected to the city by a mole, which Khizr (Barbarossa) had ordered constructed after the capture of the Peñon in 1529 (as de Sosa notes).[8] Both de Sosa and d'Aranda agree on the length of the mole: three hundred paces—about 750 feet (228 meters). The mole formed a breakwater, which in turn formed the harbor. Here is Mascarenhas' description: "The Mole is very well constructed, so high that it covers the tops of the ships it houses, and so big that every ship can moor close enough to it to store ballast, artillery, and barrels of water on the Mole itself and still leave plenty of room for people to pass."

The city of Algiers, remember, was protected by an encircling, defensive wall studded with towers. According to de Sosa, the wall was thirty spans high and twelve thick. A "span" is a handspan (the distance between the outstretched thumb

---

8. The standard definition of such a "mole" is "a wall, usually made of stone, that extends into the sea and encloses or protects a harbor."

and little finger), normally considered to be about 9 inches (23 centimeters), so by this measurement the wall would have been a little over 22 feet (7 meters) high and about 9 feet (almost 3 meters) thick. There was a dry moat outside it, though both de Sosa and d'Aranda comment on how poorly it was kept up (de Sosa: "very blocked up with dirt, trash, and infinite filth"; d'Aranda: "full of filth and ill kept"). Mascarenhas observes: "The Algiers wall is made of stone and lime, and partly of lime bricks, but it is very old and very fragile." Despite these shortcomings, the wall/moat combination must have constituted a formidable enough defense against most things except cannon fire.

By de Sosa's and d'Aranda's figures, the area the wall enclosed would be something near 50 acres, though some modern estimates put it at closer to 70 acres. Whatever the actual size, within the walls, the city was crowded. De Sosa estimates the population in terms of households: "the number of houses included within the circuit of its walls comes to some 12,200 large and small." Dan does the same, though he comes up with a different number (perhaps because he is writing a half century later): "If one were to count all the houses of Algiers, one would end up with at least around fifteen thousand, in which five or six households sometimes live in a single dwelling." He has this to say about the overall population: "Many assured me that this city has a population of over one hundred thousand inhabitants, Turks, Moors, Janissaries, slaves, and Jews." Despite his different count for houses, d'Aranda's overall population estimate is the same: "The hundred thousand souls which inhabit this city are divided into twelve thousand soldiers, Turks belonging to the Garrison, thirty or forty thousand slaves of all nations, and the rest Citizens of Algiers, Moors, Moriscos, Jews, and some Christian merchants." According to d'Aranda, "the want of room has forced them to build houses on the ramparts, which serve for one side of walls. The streets are very narrow, and are chained up at night, save only the principal street, which runs across the City." De Sosa's comment is this: "Neither a horseman nor two people walking side by side could pass through them [the streets] easily. The entire city is so dense, and the houses so close to each other, that it all seems like a very tight pine cone."

Several streets running from the major gates down to the center of Al-Wata were more than mere alleyways, but the principal street that d'Aranda mentions was by far the widest. De Sosa estimates its width at 40 spans, or about 30 feet (9 meters). It transected the city, running parallel with the waterfront. The souks (markets) were laid out along it, including the slave market (known as the Batistan) where the Icelanders were auctioned off.[9] It derived its name from these souks: the Great Street of the Souk (Al-Souk al-Kabir). Two of the main gates were located at either end of Al-Souk al-Kabir: the Gate of the River (Bab al-Oued) at the northern end, and the Gate of Grief (Bab Azzoun) at the southern. Captives were marched publically along Al-Souk al-Kabir to the Batistan to be sold.

Aside from the mass of private dwellings, there were a number of public buildings. Mosques dotted the city, including the Great Mosque (Djama'a al-Kebir), built at the end of the eleventh century and located near the waterfront, and the Ketchaoua Mosque (Djama'a Ketchaoua), built in 1612 in the heart of Al-Wata. Both were standing in Reverend Ólafur's time and are still there today. There was also the residence of the Ottoman governor of the city, located on Al-Souk al-Kabir. D'Aranda calls this building the Bassa's Palace and describes it

9. "Batistan" is also sometimes spelled "badistan" or "badestan."

as "a public structure for those who are advanced to that charge [i.e., the position of governor], well built after the modern way of Architecture." Dan describes it as follows: "The most beautiful house in Algiers is that of Bacha [Bassa], or Viceroy, which is almost in the middle of the city.... [It has] two small galleries one above the other, supported by a double row of columns of marble and porphyry." Algiers contained several large public baths, which the citizens apparently used on a regular basis. It also held the *bagnios*, where the slaves were kept.[10] Here is what de Sosa has to say of these bagnios:

The Bagnios are the houses—or, more accurately the corrals—where they keep their Christian captives and slaves. One is called the Great Bagnio, which is constructed as a square, although not exactly, since it is longer than it is wide: seventy feet long and forty feet wide. The Great Bagnio has upper and lower quarters, with many small rooms, and in the middle a cistern of water. And to one side, on the lower level, is a church or chapel for the Christians.... The other bagnio, called the Bagnio de la Bastarda, is not as large but is also divided into many habitations.... There are kings... who keep sometimes fifteen hundred to two thousand Christians in that Bagnio of the King, whereas the captives in the Bagnio de la Bastarda ordinarily number no more than four or five hundred.

We now have a clearer sense of what seventeenth century Algiers was like: a modestly sized (by modern standards) harbor

10. There are various explanations for the use of the term "bagnio" (or "bagno") to denote slave prisons. One is that the prison in Constantinople where hostages were kept was located near a public bathhouse, and the term came into general use throughout the Ottoman Empire to designate any prison. Another is that the dungeon in the Livorno castle was called the bagno because it was located below the level of the sea. Turkish slaves were kept there, and so the term became used generally to denote a prison. Whatever the derivation, the connection with "bath" (Latin, *balneum*; Turkish, *banyo*; Spanish, *baño*; Italian, *bagno*; French, *bain*) is clear enough.

*Algerii Saracenorum urbis fortissimae,*
Chorographic view of Algiers

city built on a hillside, surrounded by a defensive wall, packed
with houses, densely populated by a mix of people of many
backgrounds. The image above and map 5 give a visual sense
of all of this.

*Algerii Saracenorum urbis fortissimae* is a chorographic view
of the city.[11] It is from volume 2 of *Civitates Orbis Terrarum* (*Cities of the World*), first published in Cologne in 1572 (volume 2
published in 1575). It is not a literally accurate map of the city,
but one can make out the mole (with ships moored to it) in the

11. This illustration derives its title from the text of the scroll in the bottom
right corner: *Algerii Saracenorum urbis fortissimae, in Numidia Africae Provincia
structae, iuxta Balearicos fluctus Maediterranei aequoris Hispaniam contra Othoma-
norum Principum imperio redactae, imago* (View of Algiers, powerful city of the
Saracens, in the African province of Numidia, beside the Balearic Current of the
Mediterranean Sea, facing Spain, under the imperial rule of the Ottomans).

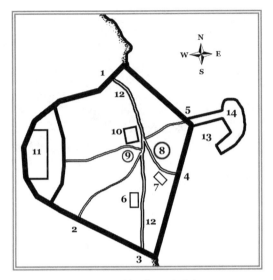

5. Topographic view of Algiers

GATES
1 Gate of the River (Bab al-Oued)
2 New Gate (Bab al-Jadid)
3 Gate of Grief (Bab Azzoun)
4 Gate of the Sea (Bab al-Bahr)
5 Gate of the Island (Bab Jazira)

BUILDINGS
6 The Great Bagnio of the Slaves (Beylik)
7 The Bagnio de la Bastarda
8 The Great Mosque (Djama'a al-Kebir)

9 Ketchaoua Mosque (Djama'a Ketchaoua)
10 Bassa's Palace (Dar al-Sultan)
11 Citadel (Al-Qasaba)

OTHER
12 Great Street of the Souk (Al-Souk al-Kabir)
13 Harbor
14 Mole

foreground, the defensive wall encircling the entire city, the wide thoroughfare of Al-Souk al-Kabir transecting the city about a third of the way up from the harbor front, and Al-Qasaba, with its own encircling wall, at the top.

The map of Algiers is a topographic view of the city and shows the walls, the main gates, main roads, and main buildings. It is not intended to be an exact, to-scale representation,

merely a schematic approximation to give the reader a simpli-
fied bird's-eye view of the seventeenth century city's geography.

The reader now has a sense of seventeenth century Algiers as a
physical place. But what about the experience of living there as
a slave?

Such an experience was, of course, traumatic. Imagine yourself dragged bodily into a marketplace in a strange, unfamiliar,
crowded city, where you understood not one word of what was
said around you, and being put up for auction. Father Dan, the
Trinitarian friar, gives us a sense of what that process of auction was like. It is worth quoting him at some length:

The place where that infamous & cursed trade [i.e., selling people into
slavery] happens in Algiers is in the midst of the city, in the Batistan
or Soc [Souk], a square with four galleries, but all uncovered, where
it is the custom to assemble as in a marketplace. Here is how they
proceed.

Recently taken captives are brought out of the prison where they
are kept under guard and brought to the Batistan, along with the
Rais, or Captains, of the vessels that have captured them, and other
officers deputized expressly, in order to ascertain how much the captives will be sold for. There are brokers, like horse dealers, who, well
versed in this business, walk beside the captives to the market, loudly
shouting that they are for sale to whoever wants to buy them. This I
have seen multiple times, with so much unhappiness that I must confess I had tears in my eyes and my heart went cold.

[In the Batistan] the buyers carefully scrutinize these poor Christian captives, whom they strip naked as they like, without regard for
their shame. No matter what, the captives must obey every command
immediately, or be struck with truncheons, which these inhuman
people are always quick to use. The buyers look to see if the captives
are strong or weak, healthy or sick, or if they have any wound, or

some disease that can prevent them from working. After this, using blows of their truncheons, the buyers make the captives walk, jump, and cavort about in order to determine how healthy they are. The buyers also look at the captives' teeth, not to know their age, but to see if they have tooth decay, which would make them less valuable. In addition, they look into the captives' eyes and study their faces in an effort to divine their natures, whether good or bad.

These slave auctions separated parents from children (as Reverend Ólafur recounts), wives from husbands, crewmates from each other, friend from friend. Once sold, the newly arrived captive became property, to be dealt with as her or his owner saw fit. If the owner was a private individual, the slave might end up as essentially a domestic servant, and the chances of ransom were apparently quite good (if the slave had access to the necessary resources). If the owner was the "bassa" (aka, the pasha, the beylerbey, the governor of the city) or the city authorities, the situation could be dire. Such slaves faced a life of hard labor, and their chances of ransom were slim. Discussing the Bagnio de la Bastarda, Mascarenhas writes: "In this Bagnio there are only slaves belonging to the city, since this prison belongs to the city. These slaves will never leave there, for they are never ransomed."

The daily life of a slave, then, depended on who the owner was. Female slaves, if not bought as concubines, were typically put into domestic service. Male slaves were either set to a variety of tasks by their owners or rented out as laborers. Father Dan provides a list of (male) slave occupations. Here is a sampling:

Those who are old or frail are employed by their owners to sell water in the city, with donkeys loaded with great skins full of water to serve the baths and workshops and other places where there are no wells. They also sell water through the streets from a large jug they carry on their shoulder. If they fail to sell as much water as their owners command, they are beaten with truncheons, without any consideration that it is not their fault.

There are others whose owners rent them out to clean up the filth outside the city and to haul away manure from the streets and the houses.

They are also those who are forced to till the land outside the city, being attached to the yoke, with a donkey or a horse, according to the pleasure or caprice of their masters.

When large stones are needed in Algiers, mainly for maintenance & rebuilding of the Mole, the slaves are forced to haul carts, heavily laden with the stone, to which they are attached by ropes. I have seen as many as forty tied to a single cart. Horses are not used for this task because the streets are too narrow, and so the carts must be drawn by these poor captives. If they do not work hard enough, they are beaten with truncheons.

The galleys, which the Algerians use for their raiding, are terrible for the poor Christian captives who are forced, by blows, to row in them. Their feet are shackled by large iron chains, and from sunrise to sunset they experience the constant drudgery of the oar.

Beyond the hard demands of daily work, slaves in Algiers also had to contend with the consequences of being "second-class citizens." Father Dan provides the following example:

When they go out into the streets, slaves must take great care not to offend the Algerians or to get too close to them. If this happens, even if inadvertently, the Algerians strike them instantly, and continue to strike as long as the passion seizes them. So slaves must always use great care when going through the streets. If they carry any burden, they call out incessantly with the following words in the language of the country: "*Balec Sid!*" which means "Guard yourself, sir!" Evenings are an especially perilous time for Christians because of the Turks and renegades coming out of taverns drunk and furious who perpetrate all manner of indignities and outrages on any slaves they encounter, kicking and punching them, or drawing the large knives they carry at their sides like swords and wounding and sometimes killing them.

Under such conditions, it is not surprising that those slaves who could, wrote letters home pleading to be ransomed. Those who could not raise the ransom money, or who could endure their circumstances no longer, tried to escape. Mascarenhas gives us a glimpse into this aspect of slave life. He ends his description of the mole with the following:

Close by [the mole] there is a small beach where, when they have finished the day's work, Christians and Moors pull up all the lesser boats in the harbor so that none are left afloat. They then attach these boats one to the other with iron chains and station fifteen or twenty Moorish guards, so that Christians cannot make off with them during the night. But this is not enough, because every year Christians steal four or five and, in complete safety, sail them to Spain. These boats are the best way to escape, as the boats constructed in the gardens, or made of leather, are very dangerous, and few who use such ever reach their destination.

One catches a sense here of the absolute desperation to escape, of slaves cobbling together boats "in the gardens" out of whatever materials lay at hand (including scraps of leather). Jón Jónsson notes in his letter, "There are some captured people here who sneak boats into the forest and eventually escape in them." He adds: "Some people grow too ambitious, though, and attempt to construct large, eight-oared boats able to hold many passengers; often, they are not able to finish building such big vessels. Some neglect to place lookouts in the trees to watch for coming people, to ensure that the sounds of the hammers will not be heard. Those that neglect this are caught, and suffer terribly."

Slaves caught trying to escape were punished severely; often, they were publically executed. Father Dan describes in excruciating detail some of the punishments meted out to slaves. We will not go into those here. It is enough to quote the telling bit of information he adds regarding the Bab al-Oued: "In front of this gate is an area that these barbarians have designated as the place to kill Christians. Many Christians have received, and are still receiving, the martyr's crown there."

Seventeenth century Algiers did offer opportunities for some slaves to achieve a better life, and some did just that, "turning Turk" and rising to positions of authority and influence. One (in)famous example is Ali Pegelin (also known as Ali Picheny, Ali Pichellin, Ali Bitchin, Ali Bitchnin), an Italian (with an original family name of something like Puccini or Piccini, perhaps from Venice) who was captured as a boy when the ship he was traveling on was taken by corsairs. He grew up in Algiers to be a Muslim and a corsair, becoming one of the principal captains (ra'is), and eventually led the *taifa*, the organization of the city's corsair captains. He amassed immense wealth, owned many slaves, and, among other things, financed the building of a mosque that one can still visit today in Algiers—known variously as the Mosque of Ali Piccinini, Mosquee Ali Bitchnin, or Djama'a Ali Bitchin.

Much of what we know of Ali Pegelin comes from Emmanuel d'Aranda, for Ali Pegelin was d'Aranda's owner. D'Aranda has this to say of him:

We were there five hundred and fifty Christian Slaves, all belonging to our Patron Ali Pegelin; yet he did not allow any one of this great number aught towards his sustenance. The only comfort we had was, that we had three hours every day allowed us to shift for our Livelihood; so that every one was to make the best advantage he could of his industry.

So it was possible, given the right chances (and the right sort of ruthlessness), for a Christian slave to rise to the very highest ranks of the Algiers world. For most slaves, though, life was grim. Many were ransomed, but, as Mascarenhas puts it, "For every one that is ransomed, more than twenty new captives arrive to take his place." The brutal reality of it all was this: tens of thousands of people lived and died miserably as slaves in Algiers—including most of the Icelanders taken in the Tyrkjaránið.

CR

The suffering endured by Christian slaves and the inhumanity and sheer brutality of the whole sordid system are undeniable, but it is also worth recalling that Algiers was more than just a cesspit of misery. As with so many things, it depended on who one was. The following extract from the diary of an Arab traveler who visited the city in 1590 reveals a very different sort of place:[12]

Algiers is a prosperous city with many souks and large numbers of soldiers. It is well fortified, with three gates and a spacious community mosque…. The harbor teems with ships whose captains are renowned for their courage, determination, and seaworthiness, far better than the captains of Constantinople…. Algiers is the best city in Africa, with a large number of buildings and extensive trade, its souks so full of merchandise and goods that it is called Little Constantinople. There is a good number of students in it … and there are more books in it than in other parts of Africa, most of them from Al-Andalus [Spain].

So Algiers in the seventeenth century was many things: a bustling port town and major trading center; the home port

12. Abu Hasan 'Ali ibn Muhammad ibn 'Ali Muhammad al-Tamjruti, "A Journey from Morocco to Istanbul and Back." From the third extract in the Translations section of *Europe through Arab Eyes, 1578–1727*, edited by Nabil Matar. See the Suggestions for Further Reading section for bibliographical details of this book.

of one of the Maghreb's most significant corsair fleets (some would say *the* most significant); a haven for expelled Moriscos; a center of learning; a polyglot, multicultural metropolis far more meritocratic than anywhere in Europe at the time—all based on an economy that depended on human slave labor to function, and that made life a veritable hell on earth for many of those enslaved there. It was, in other words, a city full of complexity and contradiction, a place where some could thrive while others sank into despair and death. Above all, perhaps, it was not a place for the weak.

### Salé

Located on the western (Atlantic) coast of what is now Morocco, slightly less than 150 miles (240 kilometers) south of the Straits of Gibraltar, Salé was just far enough away from the centers of conflict in the Mediterranean that it had a history different from that of other corsair cities. Unlike Algiers, it never became a sanjak (province) of the Ottoman Empire. It was also never assaulted by the Spanish during their period of expansion into the Maghreb in the early decades of the sixteenth century. Added to this, Morocco was in turmoil at the end of the sixteenth and the first part of the seventeenth centuries, with a series of contending factions warring for dominance and no central authority exerting control over the country. Together, these circumstances created a situation which allowed seventeenth century Salé its own unique set of options.

Salé's origins go back to Roman times and beyond. For our purposes, though, we only need to pick up the city's history from the sixteenth century onwards. During that century, Salé was a small city of 3,000 to 4,000 inhabitants on the north bank of the Bou Regreg river, which flows westwards into the Atlantic. The south bank held only the remains of an old fort (*Ribat* in Arabic). Early in the seventeenth century the city's

View of Salé from the sea

demographic changed dramatically when a large Muslim group of exiles from Hornachos (located in Extremadura, in the western part of southern Spain, near the border with Portugal), came to settle in Salé. For whatever reasons, the residents of Salé apparently did not find these new immigrants to their liking, and forced them to locate across the river on the south bank, where they rebuilt the Ribat. The Ribat was also known as Al-Qasaba (the Fort), and so that area came to be known as the Kasbah. As part of the continuing expulsion of Moriscos from Spain, a second, larger wave of immigrants followed the Hornachos, this time from Andalusia, in southern Spain. Whereas the Hornachos had been Arabic speaking, these new arrivals spoke Hispano-Arabic or Spanish. Neither the original residents of Salé nor the Hornachos accepted these Andalusian Moriscos, so they were forced to settle in their own area on the south bank of the river beyond the Kasbah, an area that came to be known as the Medina. The image above shows the walled town of Salé on the left, the mouth of the Bou Regreg river where it feeds into the sea, and the tower and walls of Al-Qasaba on the right.

178

So the seventeenth century city of Salé was in fact composed of three separate parts: the old and established town of Salé on the north bank of the Bou Regreg river, the Kasbah (inhabited by the Hornachos) on the south bank, and the Medina (inhabited by the Andalusian Moriscos) beyond the Kasbah, also on the south bank.[13] The different groups of Saletians could agree on very little, and there was pretty much constant strife between them. The only thing they all had in common was their mutual hatred of Spain.

Map 6 shows the layout of this three-part city. Like the topographical map of Algiers above, it is not intended to be an exact, to-scale representation, merely a schematic approximation to give the reader a bird's-eye view of the seventeenth century city's geography.

There were several corsair ports on Morocco's Atlantic coast, but by the middle of the second decade of the seventeenth century, the Spanish had attacked most of them, flushing out the resident corsairs.[14] These corsairs, mostly European renegados, then settled in Salé.

It is in this context that Salé took on its identity as a corsair capital. The Hornachos had brought wealth with them from Spain. The Andalusians had the manpower and a thirst for revenge. Salé itself had an ideal location on the Atlantic, far enough away that it was not an irresistibly tempting target to the European powers, yet close enough to make it an effective base for corsair operations. The combination of Hornacho

13. The modern-day city still reflects these divisions and is composed of two sections on either side of the Bou Regreg. The part of the city on the north bank is called Salé; the part on the south bank is called Rabat (ar-Ribaaṭ in Arabic, derived from the Ribat, the original fort that had once stood there). The city itself as a whole is now called Rabat or Rabat-Salé.

14. The closest the Spanish came to Salé was Mamora, present-day Mehdya, also known as Al-Ma'mura ("the well-populated"), about 25 miles (40 kilometers) north up the coast from Salé.

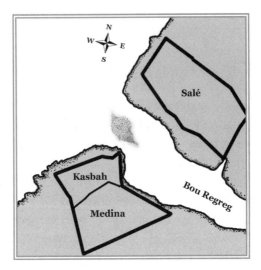

6. Topographic view of Salé

finance, Andalusian Morisco manpower, renegado ships and expertise, and effective location led to Salé becoming a formidable corsair capital, rivaling Algiers itself for a time. Salé had a shallow harbor, with a sandbar across it (see map 6), which meant large ships could not operate out of it. In its heyday, though, the port boasted a fleet of perhaps as many as fifty corsair ships, small, fast, and maneuverable, sailing in "wolf packs" that harried the Atlantic coasts of Europe for years.

Sometime in the late 1620s, the city of Salé declared its complete independence, an act it could only get away with because of the lack of any overall authority at the time in topsy-turvy Morocco. Salé then became a kind of republic, governed by a council and an elected "admiral." It is commonly believed that the first such admiral was Murat Reis—the very same Murat Reis who is thought to have masterminded the Tyrkjaránið.

The ongoing factionalism of the various groups in the city

never resolved itself, however, and the situation was far from stable, devolving into open warfare at points. By the end of the 1660s Salé was totally controlled by Sultan Al-Rashid of the Alaouite dynasty (which still rules Morocco today), and the city's days of independence were over forever.

We know far less about Salé than about Algiers. It is clear Salé was a smaller city, the seventeenth century population probably never much more than 15,000 to 20,000 people. Life for a Christian slave was no worse in Salé than in Algiers, though certainly no better. Slaves were employed in similar kinds of brute labor, treated with similar cruelty, and, like all other Maghrebi slaves, lived in constant, fervent hope of eventual ransom and liberation.

# The Icelandic Background

## A Brief History

Iceland was first settled in the second half of the ninth century by Vikings, whose descendants live there still. The island is known as the land of ice and fire—of glaciers and volcanos. There are a dozen or so sizable glaciers. Vatnajökull, the biggest of them, is the world's third largest ice sheet (after Greenland and Antarctica), with ice up to a kilometer thick. Depending on how one counts them, the island contains about 130 volcanoes (active and inactive), and eruptions have been constant (though intermittent) events throughout the centuries. Iceland lies just south of the Arctic Circle, but thanks to the moderating effect of the Gulf Stream, among other things, its climate is milder than one would expect. Present-day winter temperatures rarely dip below 15 Fahrenheit (−10 Celsius) and summer temperatures can reach 70 Fahrenheit (21 Celsius) or higher. Because of the latitude, the amount of daylight varies dramatically with the seasons: the short winter days are only four hours long; long summer days are up to twenty-one hours. Iceland is a land of contrasts, of darkness and light, stormy coasts and inland deserts, glaciers and volcanos, a land of stark, surprising beauty—and not at all an easy place to live without the support of modern technology. Iceland today is a contemporary European country, a thriving democracy with a high standard of living. In Reverend Ólafur's day, however, it was a very different place.

For one thing, it was colder. The so-called Little Ice Age—a period of colder temperatures that lasted several centuries—was in progress. There is no clear consensus on any exact chronology for the Little Ice Age (it is variously dated at 1300–1850, 1500–1850, 1550–1850, 1600–1900), but there is pretty general agreement that the period from the middle of the sixteenth to the middle of the seventeenth centuries was one of significantly colder temperatures than today. Among other things, this meant a shorter growing season. In a place like Iceland, that could be dire.

Iceland also suffered from natural calamities. There were no less than sixteen separate volcanic eruptions in the seventeenth century—including Katla (near the south coast across from the Westman Islands) in 1625, and Grímsfjall (in the southeast) in 1629, just before and just after Reverend Ólafur's ordeal. During the fifteenth and sixteenth centuries, there were recurrent epidemics of smallpox. Famine was common. Bubonic Plague reached the island in the early fifteenth century, having the same devastating effect there as it did elsewhere. Estimates are that it killed a third or more of the population. At that time, Iceland was economically dependent on trade with Norway, but the plague struck Norway, too, and trade was crippled, leaving the Icelanders, who lacked forests of their own from which to build ships, in a dangerously precarious position.

The political system offered little help or stability during all this. Iceland became a Danish possession by the end of the fourteenth century, but the Danish merchants and traders pursued their own fortunes ruthlessly and reduced the Icelanders to further poverty. In the mid-sixteenth century, the Lutheran king of Denmark eliminated the Icelandic Catholic church, kidnapping one of its two bishops, Ögmundur Pálsson, and bringing him to Denmark, where he died; beheading the other, Jón Arason; and arrogating the Church's wealth to himself.

In Reverend Ólafur's day, the climate was cold—in the early part of the seventeenth century, Iceland experienced a series of terrible winters, during which thousands of people starved to death—but things had begun to improve economically, at least a little. In the early fifteenth century, first English and then German (from the Hanseatic League) traders had appeared, looking for cod. This precipitated a sometimes violent rivalry that lasted the better part of a century, but their presence did help boost the floundering Icelandic economy. By the close of that century, Denmark had regained control of the Icelandic fisheries, and some semblance of commercial order was restored. There were, however, pirate attacks to contend with, not only the corsair raid but also forays by Spanish and English pirates.

During all this, the Icelandic people survived as best they could. Lacking forests or hewable stone, they built their houses out of chunks of lava, layers of turf, and driftwood. In the summers they fished, farmed what they could, tended cattle and sheep. They spent the long, dark winters in their farmhouses, carding wool, making repairs, and reading to each other from the sagas by the light of flickering oil lamps (Icelanders have a long tradition of literacy). In a good year, fish and mutton and garden vegetables might be plentiful. Good year or bad, though, nearly everything else had to be imported. Estimates are that during Reverend Ólafur's day, the population of Iceland was perhaps 50,000 hardy souls.

### Icelandic Names

No introduction to Iceland would be complete without a brief discussion of Icelandic names. Icelanders do not generally use family names. Instead, they employ patronymics and matronymics. That is, Icelanders are named after their father or mother. The second name (what in other countries would be the family name) of male Icelanders typically ends in the suffix *-son* (son); the second name of female Icelanders typically ends with the suffix *-dóttir* (daughter). Hence Reverend Ólafur Egilsson's name means Ólafur the son of Egil. The name of his wife, Þorgerður Ólafsdóttir, means Þorgerður daughter of Ólaf.

For non-Icelanders, this naming system can sometimes seem confusing. Imagine a married couple who have two children, a boy and a girl. The husband might be named, say, Halldór Baldursson (Halldór son of Baldur), the wife Guðrún Jónsdóttir (Guðrún daughter of Jón). Their son might be named Einar, which would make him Einar Halldórsson (Einar son of Halldór). Their daughter might be named Helga, which would make her Helga Halldórsdóttir (Helga daughter of Halldór). But the son (particularly in modern Iceland) might equally be named Einar Guðrúnarson (Einar son of Guðrún) and the daughter Helga Guðrúnardóttir (Helga daughter of Guðrún). So in what is otherwise a familiarly classic two-parent/two-child nuclear family, each member would have a different name. Some names stay in families for generations, too, and children are quite often named after their grandmothers and grandfathers. Men, in particular, often have the same name as their grandfathers, so the male lineage of our imaginary family might go like this: grandfather: Baldur Halldórsson; father: Halldór Baldursson; grandson: Baldur Halldórsson.

Icelandic names are further complicated by Icelandic grammar. Unlike English, Icelandic declines its nouns. Icelandic nouns have four cases: nominative (subjective case in English), accusative (direct object in English), dative (indirect object in English), and genitive (possessive in English). Not only are nouns declined; people's names are declined as well. Reverend Ólafur's name, for instance, has four forms: Ólafur (nominative), Ólaf (accusative), Ólafi (dative), and Ólafs (genative). We have chosen to use the nominative case form of his name throughout. However, Icelandic patronymic/matronmymic names employ the genitive form. So if Reverend Ólafur had a son named Egil, that son's name would not be Egil Ólafursson. It would be Egil Ólafsson—"Ólafs" (genitive) plus "son" (same word as in English). This is why Reverend Ólafur's daughter's name was Helga Ólafsdóttir —"Ólafs" (genitive) plus "dóttir" (daughter in English).

## The Westman Islands (Vestmannaeyjar)

The Westman Islands are an archipelago of small islands off the south coast of Iceland. Only the largest, Heimaey (pronounced "Hay-mah-ay"), is permanently inhabited. Heimaey was first peopled by Norse settlers (Vikings) around 900 AD. These Vikings brought Irish thralls (slaves) with them when they settled Iceland. The story has it that some of these Irish slaves killed the blood-brother of Ingólfur Arnarson, one of Iceland's first settlers, and fled to the islands, where Ingólfur found them and killed them in revenge. Since Ireland is west of Scandinavia, the Vikings called the Irish the Westmen—and so the islands got their name.

There were extremely rich fishing grounds around Heimaey, and the island had a good natural harbor. This was an attractive combination. In the late fifteenth century, the English built a fort at the harbor entrance on Heimaey and ruled the area by force until they were eventually ousted by the Danish in the mid-sixteenth century. In 1602, a Danish trading monopoly was established, and only Danish merchants had the right to trade on Heimaey. In 1609, the king of Denmark claimed the Westman Islands, so in Reverend Ólafur's day they were a Danish royal possession administered by Danish factors— hence the Danish trading houses at the harbor.

The inhabitants of the island survived by fishing, subsistence farming, hunting seabirds, and collecting seabird eggs. In

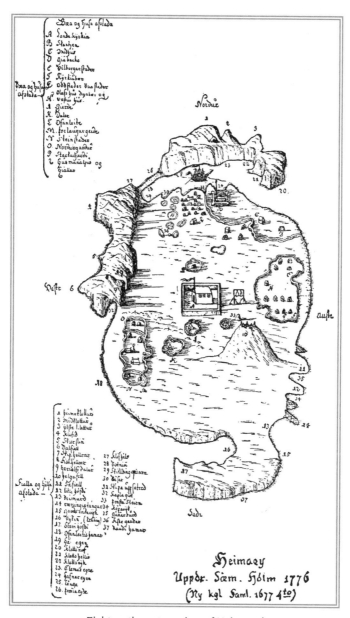

7. Eighteenth century view of Heimaey by
Sæmundur Magnússon Hólm

Reverend Ólafur's time, there were about eighteen farmsteads, with livestock, and forty houses without livestock. An estimated four hundred to five hundred people lived on the island at the time of the corsair raid. This gives a sense of the scale of the tragedy: the corsairs killed somewhere between thirty and forty people and took away two hundred and forty-two, men, women, and children. Basically, they depopulated the island. Barbary corsairs were not the only ones to raid Heimaey. In 1614, for instance, a pirate ship captained by a James (John) Gentleman, from Southwold, England, plundered the island. The result was not as calamitous as the Tyrkjaránið, since his men did not kill or kidnap people, but they stole everything they could, including the church bell of Landakirkja church.

## Reverend Ólafur

Reverend Ólafur Egilsson was born in 1564 (though the date is not absolutely certain), on a farm in Snorrastaðir, in Laugardalur, in South Iceland (see map 8, Southwest Iceland, for this and other locations relating to Reverend Ólafur). Icelanders keep meticulous genealogical records, so his family details are clear. He was the son of Egill Einarsson, a farmer in Snorrastaðir. Egill, in turn, was the son of Reverend Einar Ólafsson, a priest at Hrepphólar and a land steward in the Skálholt episcopal see.[1] Reverend Ólafur's mother was Katrín Sigmundsdóttir. Her grandfather was Reverend Sigmundur Eyjólfsson, a priest in Hítardal (located just north of the territory covered by the map). Sigmundur was consecrated as bishop of Skálholt see in Trondheim, Norway, in 1537, but he died a few weeks later. Sigmundur's mother was Ásdís Pálsdóttir, sister of Ögmundur Pálsson, the last Catholic bishop of Skálholt see. Rev-

1. Skálholt was the bishop's see for all of Iceland except the north, where the see was at Hólar. Established in 1056, Skálholt remained the center of both ecclesiastical and political affairs until the end of the eighteenth century.

8. Southwest Iceland

erend Ólafur was thus closely connected to the final generation of Iceland's Catholic clergy.

Reverend Ólafur was ordained as a priest at Torfastaðir church farm (close to Skálholt and Snorrastaðir, where he was born) in 1592. Later that same year, he was ordained in Ofan-leiti parish on the Westman Islands. At that time, the Westman Islands had only one major church, the Landakirkja church. This was a large wooden structure. It needed to be big to accommodate the migratory population of fishermen from the mainland who lived on the island during the fishing season. Though there was just the one large church, there were two pastors and two parishes, one at Kirkjubær and one at Ofanleiti (see map 2, showing the sea and land routes of the Barbary corsairs at Heimaey, for the locations of these parishes). Reverend Jón Þorsteinsson was installed at Kirkjubær, and Reverend Ólafur at Ofanleiti. Kirkjubær had a chapel, Ofanleiti a little church. Ofanleiti parish was a *beneficium*. It contained a farmstead—owned by the church and under the control of the bishop at Skálholt—that was rented out to the resident pastor, who did not receive any payment but had to live off the revenue of the farm, like other farmers.

Reverend Ólafur was married twice. His first wife was Helga Árnasdóttir.[2] They had one daughter, Þorgerður Ólafsdóttir. Þorgerður married Reverend Gísli Þorvarðsson, who was a priest in Ofanleiti on the Westman islands from 1627 to 1636. Reverend Ólafur's second wife was Ásta (pronounced "Owstah") Þorsteinsdóttir. Her father was Reverend Þorsteinn Einarsson, a priest at Mosfell (located a little north of modern-day Reykjavík). Her mother was Guðrún Þorsteinsdóttir. Guðrún was the sister of Reverend Jón Þorsteinsson, the other pastor on Heimaey, who was killed during the corsair raid. (In Icelandic history, Reverend Jón is known as Jón Þorsteinsson the Martyr.) Reverend Ólafur and Ásta had four children. The eldest was Helga Ólafsdóttir. She was not captured in the raid and married Finnur Guðmundsson of Snjallsteinshöfði farm. The three younger children—an eleven-year-old boy, a two-year-old, and an infant born on the voyage to Algiers—were taken in the raid, along with Reverend Ólafur and his wife, and sold into slavery. He never saw any of these children again. His wife, however, was among the Icelanders who were finally ransomed and brought back to Iceland a decade after the raid.

We do not know much about Ásta. We do, however, have the record of her ransom payment:[3]

2. All we know about Helga Árnasdóttir is that she married Reverend Ólafur and gave birth to a daughter. Presumably she must have died in order for Reverend Ólafur to remarry (divorce would not have been an option), but there is nothing further about her in the records.

3. This ransom record is given in the 1906–9 edition of *Tyrkjaránið á Íslandi 1627* (*The Turkish Raid in Iceland 1627*). The ransom expedition was a complicated affair. The "project manager" was Paul de Willum (also de Willumis), working on

Gekofft vonn Aille Pitterlingk Cilleby: 2 frouwenn tho weiter
Aster torstiens dress Presters frouwe vud gnudele hermanns

|  | Costen alle beyde | Rd. 500:– |
|  | Portgellt | Rd. 134:– |
|  |  | Rd. 634: – |

Bought from Aille Pitterlingk Cilleby: 2 women,
Ásta Þorsteinsdóttir, the Pastor's wife, and Gunnhildur Hermannsdóttir.

|  | Cost all paid: | Rigsdaler 500:– |
|  | Port tax: | Rigsdaler 134:– |
|  | Total | Rigsdaler 634:– |

According to the ransom records, Ásta was one of the most expensive captives to free. She cost 400 rigsdaler (see the Currencies section in this appendix for a discussion of Danish currency). Gunnhildur's price was a more ordinary 100 rigsdaler. The prices for other captives on the list ranged from 43 rigsdaler up to, occasionally, as much as 225 rigsdaler. The other thing to note here is that "Aille Piterlingk," the man they were bought from, is no doubt Ali Pegelin, the same man who owned Emmanuel d'Aranda and (according to d'Aranda) 550 other slaves. The above, and the fact that Ásta lived on for thirty years after her husband's death, are about all we know of her.

Reverend Ólafur returned to Iceland on July 6, 1628—almost exactly one year after the raid—and resumed living on Heimaey. Though he did not have any official post as a clergyman for nearly a decade, he received financial support (one-third of the income from both of the parishes on the island) until he regained his old office in Ofanleiti parish in 1636. Ásta,

---

behalf of the Danish Crown, who made use of the extensive Dutch trade network and trade connections in Marseilles. De Willum signed the ransom receipts. The total cost (including ransoms and all other expenses) was 16,687 rigsdalers—a colossal sum by Icelandic standards at the time.

joined him there after she was successfully ransomed in that year. The two were able to live together for nearly three full years before Reverend Ólafur died on March 1, 1639, at the age of seventy-five. After her husband's death, Ásta left Heimaey and went to live with her surviving daughter, Helga, and her son-in-law at their farm in Snjallsteinsshöföi. She lived there until she died.

Little is known of Reverend Ólafur Egilsson himself except what can be gleaned from *The Travels*, where he appears as an intelligent, devout, literate man, though also a man of somewhat limited experience. A rural clergyman cast out roughly into the wider world, he must have been a resilient and adaptable person, for, though he was in his sixties when he underwent his ordeal, he handled the harrowing situations he found himself in sufficiently well that he lived to write about the experience.

## Currencies and Distances

Reverend Ólafur uses terms for currencies and distances that would have been familiar to his Icelandic readers, but are not so today. Understanding these terms helps the reader relate more easily to his experiences.

### Currencies

Seventeenth century coinage was eccentric and confusing by modern standards. None of the multiple currencies in use was decimal. Instead, they derived in varying degrees from the Carolingian monetary system established during the end of the eighth and beginning of the ninth centuries during the reigns of Pepin the Short and his son Charlemagne the Great. This system, in turn, was derived from the currency used in the Eastern Roman Empire, centered at Byzantium. Carolingian currency consisted of *livre* (Latin, *libra*), *sou* or *sol* (Latin, *solidus*), and *denier* (Latin, *denarius*). The Carolingian livre (French for "pound") literally referred to a pound weight.[4] The weight of the Carolingian silver denier coin was such that 240 deniers could be struck from a pound of silver. This is the genesis of the eccentric ratio of traditional English coinage (1 pound = 20 shillings = 240 pence) and of other coinages like the French (1 livre = 20 sou = 240 deniers) and Italian (1 *lire* = 20 = *soldi* = 240 *denari*). The Carolingian livre/sou/denier system was notional, however. It specified relative values rather than coins in circulation. The only Carolingian coins actually struck were silver deniers (silver pennies).

By the seventeenth century, the Carolingian system had devolved into a myriad local currencies as individual countries and kingdoms—sometimes individual districts or even towns—minted a bewildering array of coins of widely varying weights and values. But there was also a theoretical system, usually termed "money of account," employed for accounting purposes that helped compensate for this pecuniary confusion. The money-of-account system used a set number of nominal coins, of a set value, to record transactions. The standard coin used in the money-of-account system might or might not exist as an actual physical coin in circulation. The French money-of-account coin, the *livre de gros tournois*, was not a circulating coin; the Dutch *gulden* was.

Seventeenth century coinage was further complicated by the fact that, like the Carolingian currency it was based on, the coins had an intrinsic value: the metal content of a particular coin determined its worth—at least in theory. Matters were also com-

4. The pound in question was a Troy pound, which contained 12 ounces. The 12-ounce pound Troy weight system, the name of which derives (probably) from the French city of Troyes (and not from the famous Troy of the *Iliad*), has been generally superseded by the avoirdupois system, the 16-ounce pound system we are now familiar with ("avoirdupois" drives from the Old French phrase *aveir de peis*, meaning "goods of weight"). The Troy system is still used to weigh precious metals.

ICELANDIC BACKGROUND

plicated by several other factors. Currencies were fundamentally bimetallic—consisting of both gold and silver coins—and there was a set ratio of value between the two metals. This ratio was not stable, however. Among other things, the huge influx of Spanish New World silver in the sixteenth century disrupted the system. Authorities revalued their currencies to reset the gold/silver ratio, but since this revaluation was a piecemeal affair, done on a country-by-country, area-by-area basis, it had an effect of setting off currency speculation. Speculators might, for example, buy silver coins in England, where the silver/gold ratio value was, say, 13:1 (that is, 13 units of silver to 1 unit of gold), and then use those same silver coins to buy gold at a profit in the Netherlands, where the silver/gold ratio might be 12:1. They could then take those gold coins back to England and buy more silver at a profit, and so on. The result of all this on an international scale was a mess, with constant revaluations, re-revaluations, and chronic shortages of coins.

Currencies were also destabilized by the long series of armed conflicts that marked the sixteenth and seventeenth centuries— the major one in Reverend Ólafur's day being the Thirty Years' War. Such conflicts could disrupt the supply of money, destroying business enterprises in the process and sending values spiraling upwards or downwards. These conflicts were also ruinously expensive, bankrupting governments and monarchs and forcing them to take sometimes extreme measures of revaluation in order to salvage their currencies.

Despite all this confusion, however, there was still what amounted to an internationally recognized currency exchange rate system, and certain coins gained wide enough recognition to become standard units that could be used for transactions between countries. The standard international gold coin derived from the Venetian *ducat* (and Florentine *florin*). In northern Europe, this gold coin became the Dutch gulden (*guilder*). The standard international silver coin was the thaler, which (theoretically) contained a weight of silver equal in value to two gold ducats/gulden.[5] The standard Spanish silver coin, known as the real de a ocho, was equal in value to the thaler, as was the Dutch silver leeuwendaalder (lion's dollar).[6]

Since Iceland was a Danish possession at the time, Reverend Ólafur would have thought in terms of Danish currency, so the "daler" he refers to in the text would be the rigsdaler, which was the Danish silver coin approximately equivalent to the thal-

5. "Thaler" is the term from which our modern "dollar" derives. The thaler derived its name from the place where it was first minted in the early sixteenth century, Joachimsthal, in Bohemia (there was a silver mine there), in what is now the Czech Republic but was then part of the Habsburg Holy Roman Empire. In German, "thal" means "valley" (the modern spelling is "tal"). In German, the suffix -er added to place names indicates residence/location in that place (as in our remnant English version: "New Yorker," i.e., somebody from New York), so "thaler" means "from the valley." Similar silver coins began to be minted in different thals (valleys) in the Holy Roman Empire, and "thaler" became the generic term for them. Eventually, one developed into a standard money-of-account coin: the *reichsthaler*. The word "thaler" had cognates in other northern European languages—*daalder* in Dutch, dalur in Icelandic, daler in Danish—and became pronounced as "dollar" in English. The Dutch daalder (specifically the *leeuwendaalder*) was equal in value to a thaler, as was the Spanish real de a ocho. Because of a shortage of official English currency in the Thirteen Colonies, the leeuwendaalder and the real de a ocho, which were stable, internationally recognized coins, were widely used. The real de a ocho was known as the Spanish "dollar" (since it was equivalent to the daalder, and any number of other "dalers"), and so common did the term become that "dollar" was adopted to designate the official unit of currency for the fledgling United States (a far more popular designation at the time than "pound"). The real de a ocho, and other foreign coins, were legal tender in the United States until 1857.

6. The real de a ocho ("real" derives from "royal," so literally "royal of eight"), also known as the peso de a ocho ("piece of eight") or more simply as the peso, was so named because it was worth 8 reales (the ordinary real being a lesser-value Spanish silver coin). There was also a real de a dos, (a double real, worth 2 ordinary reales) and a real de a cuatro (a quadruple real, worth 4 ordinary reales). The real de a ocho is the (in)famous "piece of eight" coin so coveted by one and all in classic pirate stories.

er, the Spanish real de a ocho, and the Dutch leeuwendaalder.[7] Danish currency consisted of mark, skilling, and *penning* (1 mark = 16 skillings = 192 pennings; 6 marks = 1 rigsdaler). When Reverend Ólafur mentions "shillings" it is these Danish skillings he would have in mind. During his travels, he could estimate the values of local prices and currencies by equating them to the internationally recognized value of the rigsdaler. He was, in other words, working out exchange rates that his readers would have been able to understand.

The ransoms payments made in order to free Christian captives were paid in internationally recognized currencies. In Algiers at the time, this seems to have been mostly reales de a ocho. The ransom paid for Ásta Þorsteinsdóttir and the other Icelanders was in rigsdalers—an acceptable currency because rigsdalers were recognized as equivalent in value to reales de a ocho.

The obvious question, of course, is this: how expensive were these ransoms? How much, exactly, was the 500 rigsdalers paid for Ásta Þorsteinsdóttir and Gunnhildur Hermannsdóttir worth in the daily life of an ordinary Icelander? By modern standards, 500 "dollars" does not seem like very much. One should not, however, equate seventeenth century dalers with modern dollars.

There is limited data on people's earnings in the early seventeenth century, but there are some records of laborers' wages in London, England. Estimates are that an average daily wage for a laborer in London in the 1620s was about 16 pennies. If (for the sake of argument) we assume a five-day week, this equates to a weekly wage of 80 pennies, or 6 shillings and 8 pennies

7. In chapter XI, Reverend Ólafur himself equates the rigsdaler to the real de a ocho: "The Turks demanded a total of twelve hundred dalers, which they call *Stück von achten* [German for 'pieces of eight']."

(12 pennies to a shilling), and an annual wage (for a 52-week year) of 4,160 pennies, or 17 pounds, 6 shillings, 8 pennies (1 pound = 20 shillings = 240 pennies). This is a theoretical estimate, of course. No laborer was likely to work continuously, for precisely five days a week, every week, for 52 weeks a year. And this wage is for laborers in London, a major metropolis, where wages would have been higher than elsewhere. Comparable wages outside London during the same time period might have amounted to no more than half that amount, making an annual wage of 8 pounds, 13 shillings and 4 pennies. Typical wages for agricultural workers would have been about the same as those for non-London laborers—that is, about 8 pennies a day, or somewhere between 8 and 9 pounds annually. All of this, of course, is only a rough estimate, and wages in England are only approximately comparable to the rest of Europe at the time. But these calculations at least give us some "ballpark" figures.

The rounded-off annual wage of a London laborer, then, would have been about 345 shillings a year. The rounded-off annual wage for a non-London laborer, or an agricultural laborer, would have been about 175 shillings a year. Since 4 English shillings were worth approximately the same as 1 rigsdaler/thaler, the annual wage for a London laborer would equal about 86 rigsdaler, while the annual wage for a non-London laborer, or an agricultural laborer, would equal about 43 rigsdaler. Even the higher annual wage is significantly less than one-fifth the sum paid to ransom Ásta Þorsteinsdóttir and Gunnhildur Hermannsdóttir, making their ransom worth more than five years' worth of wages if the wage-earner was well paid, and more than ten years' worth of wages if the wage-earner was an ordinary laborer or farm hand—as the vast majority of people were. The 1,200 (rigs)daler ransom demanded for Reverend Ólafur's wife and children represented no less than fourteen years' worth of wages at the well-paid scale and twenty-eight years' worth of wages for an ordinary laborer or farmhand.

English wages might in a general way be comparable to continental European wages at the time, but they certainly were not comparable to Icelandic wages. In the seventeenth century, Iceland was a poor country with no cities, little farming, and an economy severely restricted by weather and isolation. Average annual wages for most people would have been substantially less than those of English agricultural laborers. A ransom amount of 500 rigsdalers, then, even if it bought the freedom of two captives, was a great deal of money indeed, far more than ordinary Icelanders were capable of coming up with. The ransom demanded for Reverend Ólafur's wife and children represented an impossible sum. Catholic captives could rely to some extent on redemption societies like the Trinitarians or the Mercedarians to raise ransom money for them. The captive Icelanders had no such redemption societies to turn to. For ordinary people like Reverend Ólafur, possessing no personal wealth, their only hope was to be redeemed by their monarch.

### Distances

As with the currency, measurement of distance in seventeenth century Europe varied considerably from country to country. European units of distance were based on measurements worked out by the Romans, but over the centuries, as individual areas adapted them to their own purposes, a wide variety of different units of measurement developed. The only one we need to concern ourselves with here is the mile.

Our modern statute mile derives from the Latin *mille passus* (one thousand paces), which is generally considered to be equal to a little less than 4,920 feet (1,500 meters), which, of course, is similar to what a statute mile is today (5,280 feet; 1,609 meters). Measurements of a "mile" in Reverend Ólafur's time, however, differed considerably from this. The early seventeenth century Spanish mile, the legua de por grado (league of the degree), equaled between 24,000 and 25,776 feet (7,315–7,857 meters), or between 4.5 and 4.8 statute miles, depending on how it was calculated. A Danish Sjællandsk mile was about 36,537 feet (11,136 meters), or 6.92 statute miles. So the "miles" mentioned in the text do not correspond to what we today think of as miles.

### The Tyrkjaránið Today

The trauma engendered by the Tyrkjaránið is long gone, but the raid remains alive in the minds of many Icelanders today. There is a museum on Heimaey, known as the 1627 Heritage Center, where visitors can view exhibits detailing the events of the raid and even take a tour of the island following the routes the corsairs took, from their landing at the strand at Brimurð on the southeast section of the island, to the caves of Fiskihellar Mountain, where Icelanders were hauled out of hiding or shot, to the rock monument marking the spot where (according to the story) one of the corsairs uncharacteristically took pity on a pregnant woman and let her alone rather than abducting her.

One hears talk in Iceland about an old law, only recently repealed, that legally permitted Icelanders to kill a "Turk" on sight, though this appears to be an urban (in this case, perhaps, rural) myth. Myth or not, the notion persists.

Icelanders keep meticulous genealogical records, and descendants of Reverend Ólafur—traced accurately generation through generation in the records from the offspring of his first wife and of his daughter who was not abducted—can be found in Iceland today. One of the people mentioned in the Acknowledgments to this book, in fact, is such a descendent. There are many.

APPENDIX C

# The Manuscript Sources

*The Travels of Reverend Ólafur Egilsson*

Reverend Ólafur completed *The Travels* shortly after he returned to Iceland in the summer of 1628. His story became very popular and was widely copied—by hand—for almost three hundred years. The original *Travels* manuscript, however, is lost, and only copies from the seventeenth and eighteenth centuries remain today. None of the existing manuscripts predates 1728. It has been suggested that all the earlier manuscripts were gathered into the collection of Árni Magnússon (1663–1730), an Icelandic scholar and keen amasser of Icelandic manuscripts, and were housed in Copenhagen but were consumed in the fire that devastated that city in 1728. Of the thirty-four manuscript copies of *The Travels* now known, twenty-eight are in the National Library of Iceland, three are in the King's Library (Royal Library) in Copenhagen, Denmark, two are in the Skógar District museum in South Iceland, and one is in the Bodleian Library in Oxford, England.

In 1906–9, two manuscripts of *The Travels* were published by Jón Þorkelsson for Sögufélagið (the Historical Society of Iceland) in a book titled *Tyrkjaránið á Íslandi 1627 (The Turkish Raid in Iceland 1627)*. This was the standard scholarly Icelandic language edition. Þorkelsson designated these two manuscripts the A-text and the B-text, the A-text having few biblical quotations, the B-text having numerous biblical quotations. The

B-text, which forms the basis of the 1906–9 published edition, is based on a manuscript known as Thott 514, which is in the Thott collection (part of the Royal Library) in Copenhagen. It is an octavo manuscript, written in 1741 by Hannes Pálsson in Hnífsdalur neðri by Skutulsfjörður, in the Westfjörds of Iceland. In 1967, the B-text (Thott 514) from the 1906–9 publication was reprinted and published, unchanged. This edition, with an extended introduction by Sverrir Kristjánsson, became the standard Icelandic language edition of *The Travels*.

More than a hundred years have passed since Þorkelsson's 1906–9 edition was published. In the ensuing time, more manuscripts have been discovered. Among them are those that Þórður Tómasson, curator of the Skógar district museum in South Iceland, has been able to find. One, written in 1850, he brought to the museum in 1938. In 1981, he acquired a handwritten octavo book started by Sigurður Magnússon in Holtum in 1779 and completed by Sighvatur Einarsson in Skálakot in 1824. This handwritten book includes two manuscript versions of *The Travels*, the first copied by Sigurður Magnússon in 1779, the second copied and slightly enlarged by Sighvatur Einarsson in 1824. The octavo book in which these manuscripts are found is designated Skógar 1981.

Jón Þorkelsson claimed that the Thott 514 manuscript is very close to Reverend Ólafur's original (though he makes no mention of what evidence he has to support this). The fact remains, however, that Reverend Ólafur's original manuscript is long gone. There is thus no single definitive text of *The Travels*. There are only copies, and copies of copies. And since several new manuscripts have come to light after the standard 1906–9/1967 Icelandic-language editions of *The Travels* were published, we consulted multiple manuscripts when putting our translation together. We relied primarily on Skógar 1981, using Thott 514 for comparisons. The Skógar manuscript is sometimes a bit shorter than the Thott, but the two are for the most part similar. Among the manuscripts we consulted was Boreal 56 in the Bodleian Library, Oxford. That manuscript adds little to other known manuscripts, but it was not among those Jón Þorkelsson studied, and we felt it should not be ignored.

*The Travels* was by no means an easy book to translate. There are what appear to be a number of transcription errors on the part of the copyists. The Icelandic used by Reverend Ólafur is often archaic, and his prose is sometimes so convoluted as to be virtually opaque. A literal, word-for-word translation would have been most difficult for the modern English reader. Instead, we have tried to make this translation as clear and readily understandable as possible, and so we stuck to the "sense" rather than the "letter" of the original texts—while, of course, keeping as close to the originals as we could. We have tried to clear up possible confusions in the text of both Reverend Ólafur's narrative and the letters that accompany it with explanatory footnotes.

### The Letters

To give a clearer sense of the Tyrkjaránið, we have included not only the full text of *The Travels* itself but also five letters, one written by a local Lögsagnari (deputy sheriff) describing the events of the raid, the others written by captives to their relatives back home. As with Reverend Ólafur's narrative, our translation of these letters focuses on conveying their content as clearly as possible rather than on a strict word-for-word rendering of the original—without, of course, straying too far from the original meaning. Our translation of these letters is based primarily on the text in the *Tyrkjaránið á Íslandi 1627*, but each letter comes from a different manuscript source.

### Kláus Eyjólfsson's Letter

Although we refer to this as a letter, it was actually a formal report tendered to the authorities.

The text comes from a manuscript in the King's Library in Copenhagen. The designation is Ny kgl. Saml. 1262. Fol bl. 53b-56a. The abbreviation Ny kgl. Saml. means New King's Library Collection.

### Guðríður Símonardóttir's Letter

The text comes from page 143 of a manuscript in the *Bréfabók Gísli biskup Oddsson* (Bishop Gisli Oddsson's collected letters), designated as AM 247, 4to bl. 143r-v. The "AM" refers to the manuscript's location (the Árni Magnússon Institute in Iceland). The abbreviation "4to" means "quarto"; "bl" means "page" ("bls." for "pages"). Gísli Oddsson (1593–1638) was Bishop of Skálholt.

### Guttormur Hallsson's Letter

The text comes from a manuscript in the collection of the Landsbókasafn (National and University Library of Iceland). The designation is 769 4to (quarto) skr. C. 1770. The number "769" is the manuscript number. The abbreviation "skr. C." means "written circa."

### Jón Jónsson's Letter

The text comes from a manuscript in the collection of the Landsbókasafn (National and University Library of Iceland). The designation is 38 Fol. The listing is accompanied by the following note: *"Fol. à þrem blöðum með hendi síra Eyjólfs Jónssonar á Völlum* (d. 1745)" (folio on three sheets of handwritten paper by Reverend Eyjólfur Jónsson at Vellir [Parish]).

Anonymous Letter

The text comes from a manuscript in the collection of the Landsbókasafn (National and University Library of Iceland). The designation is 72. 4to (quarto), pages 661–67. The listing is accompanied by the following note: "Skrifað af Jóni Halldórsni í Hítardal [copied out by Jón Halldórsson in Hítardalur] c. 1720." There is also a Latin version in the *Historia ecclesiastica Islandiæ* (*Ecclesiastical History of Iceland*) by Finni Jonannæi (1775), pages 138–44.

APPENDIX D

# The Times

Reverend Ólafur Egilsson (1564–1639) is a familiar figure in Icelandic history. Outside Iceland, however, he is not so well known, and few non-Icelanders have ever read *The Travels*. The events depicted in *The Travels* occurred almost four centuries ago. Much has changed in the world since then, and some aspects of the book may seem a little puzzling to the modern secular reader.

Like people everywhere, Reverend Ólafur was a man of his times, and what he experienced, the sense he made of those experiences, and *The Travels* itself are all better understood if placed in a wider historical context.

---

Perhaps the best way to begin setting that historical context is with some names. Look at the list below. Everybody on the list was alive during Reverend Ólafur's lifetime:

Michelangelo (1475–1564)
John Calvin (1509–1564)
Gerardus Mercator (1512–1594)
Pieter Brueghel the Elder (1525–1569)
Michel de Montaigne (1533–1592)
Sir Francis Drake (1540–1596)
Tycho Brahe (1546–1601)
Miguel de Cervantes (1547–1616)
Giordano Bruno (1548–1600)
Edmund Spenser (1552–1599)
Matteo Ricci (1552–1610)
Francis Bacon (1561–1626)
Christopher Marlowe (1564–1593)
William Shakespeare (1564–1616)

Galileo Galilei (1564–1642)
Henry Hudson (c.1565–1611)
Caravaggio (1571–1610)
Johannes Kepler (1571–1630)
John Donne (1572–1631)
Ben Jonson (1572–1637)
Samuel de Champlain (1574–1635)
Peter Paul Rubens (1577–1640)
William Harvey (1578–1657)
John Smith (1580–1631)
Bishop James Ussher (1581–1656)
Frans Hals (1582–1666)
Cardinal Richelieu (1585–1642)
Thomas Hobbes (1588–1679)
René Descartes (1596–1650)
Anthony van Dyck (1599–1641)
Oliver Cromwell (1599–1658)
Velázquez (1599–1660)

Rembrandt van Rijn (1606–1669)
John Milton (1608–1674)
Sir William Penn (1621–1670)
Molière (1622–1673)
Blaise Pascal (1623–1662)
Gian Domenico Cassini (1625–1712)
Robert Boyle (1627–1691)
John Bunyan (1628–1688)
Charles Perrault (1628–1703)
Christiaan Huygens (1629–1695)
John Dryden (1631–1700)
John Locke (1632–1704)
Antonie van Leeuwenhoek (1632–1723)
Jan Vermeer (1632-1675)
Baruch Spinoza (1632–1677)
Christopher Wren (1632–1723)
Samuel Pepys (1633–1703)
Increase Mather (1639–1723

Notice that Reverend Ólafur was born in the same year as Christopher Marlowe, William Shakespeare, and Galileo Galilei—fairly illustrious company.

Reverend Ólafur lived in what is usually known as the early modern period of European history. The fact that there are so many famous names from this period is no coincidence. It was a turbulent time, a time of change in every possible way: religious, social, political, philosophical, technological. New discoveries and new ideas were everywhere. Look at the following brief list of events and publications, all of which also occurred in Reverend Ólafur's lifetime:

1610 Galileo observed the moons of Jupiter with his telescope

1611 King James Bible was published

**1618** Johannes Kepler published the *Epitome Astronomiae Copernicanae* (*Summary of Copernican Astronomy*), in which he presented the laws describing planetary motion, and so put the Copernican heliocentric view of the universe on a solid mathematical footing

**1618–1648** Thirty Years' War

**1620** Puritans founded the Plymouth, Massachusetts, colony

**1620** Francis Bacon published the *Novum Organum* (*The New Instrument, or True Directions Concerning the Interpretation of Nature*), in which he worked out the outline of the scientific method as we know it

**1627** Johannes Kepler published the *Tabulae Rudolphinae* (*The Rudolphine Tables*), a compilation of star charts used, among other purposes, for navigation

**1628** William Harvey published *Exercitatio Anatomica de Motu Cordis et Sanguinis in Animalibus* (*An Anatomical Exercise on the Motion of the Heart and Blood in Living Beings*), in which he described the circulation of blood in living creatures

**1627** Francis Bacon published *The New Atlantis*, a fictional account of an imaginary society founded on the principles he espoused in the *Novum Organum*

**1632** Galileo published *Dialogo sopra i due massimi sistemi del mondo* (*Dialogue Concerning the Two Chief World Systems*), in which he championed the Copernican heliocentric view of the universe against the traditional Ptolemaic geocentric view

**1637** René Descartes published *Discours de la méthode* (*Discourse on Method*), in which he presented his famous dictum, *cogito ergo sum* ("I think, therefore I am")

Notice that this list tends to divide itself into two sections: religious and scientific (though science would have been termed "natural philosophy" at the time). The publication of the King James Bible, the Mayflower pilgrims landing at Plymouth Rock, the Thirty Years' War—these all resulted, one way or another, from religious change (though the Thirty Years' War involved vastly more than just religion). Galileo's observing the moons of Jupiter with his telescope, along with the publication of Bacon's *Novum Organum*, of Kepler's *Epitome Astronomiae*, of Harvey's *Exercitatio anatomica*, of Galileo's *Dialogo*, and of Descartes' *Discours*, represent seminal developments in the history of science. One of the aspects of the early modern period that made it so turbulent was that these two forces—the religious and the scientific—were, in a sense, pulling in opposite directions.

## Religion

The early modern period was marked by dramatic events, not least among which was the profound religious upheaval of the Reformation and the Counter-Reformation—the emergence of Protestantism and the Catholic Church's reaction against it. The following is a brief list of some major Reformation and Counter-Reformation events:

**1517 (47 years before Reverend Ólafur's birth)** Martin Luther nailed his ninety-five theses to the door of the Castle Church in Wittenberg—precipitating the Protestant Reformation (Luther died in 1546, 18 years before Reverend Ólafur was born)

**1526 (38 years before Reverend Ólafur's birth)** William Tyndale published the first English translation of the New Testament

**1534 (30 years before Reverend Ólafur's birth)** Ignatius of Loyola (San Ignacio de Loyola) founded the Jesuits (the Society of Jesus) as part of the Catholic Counter-Reformation

**1534 (30 years before Reverend Ólafur's birth)** King Henry VIII separated from Rome and founded the Protestant Church of England

1535 (29 years before Reverend Ólafur's birth) Myles Coverdale completed William Tyndale's translation of the Old Testament and published the Coverdale Bible—the first English translation of the entire Bible

1536 (28 years before Reverend Ólafur's birth) Christian III, king of Denmark and Norway, established the state Lutheran Church in Denmark

1541 (23 years before Reverend Ólafur's birth) John Calvin returned to Geneva and began his ministry there

1545–63 (starting 19 years before Reverend Ólafur's birth) Council of Trent rejected Protestant doctrines and reaffirmed the traditional articles of Catholic faith

1550 (14 years before Reverend Ólafur's birth) Jón Arason, last Catholic bishop of Iceland, was beheaded

1555 (9 years before Reverend Ólafur's birth) Peace of Augsburg guaranteed German princes the right to determine the religion (Catholic or Lutheran) of the territory they ruled

1556 (8 years before Reverend Ólafur's birth) Geneva Bible was published (first Bible with chapter and verse numbers)

1564 (the year Reverend Ólafur was born) John Calvin died

August, 1572 (when Reverend Ólafur was 8) Saint Bartholomew's Day massacre occurred, in which perhaps as many as 100,000 Huguenots were killed in France

1598 (when Reverend Ólafur was 34) Edict of Nantes was issued, providing French Huguenots with limited protections

1611 (when Reverend Ólafur was 47) King James Bible was published

1618 (when Reverend Ólafur was 54) Thirty Years' War began

The clash between the Protestant and Catholic faiths was political and military as well as religious, and it led to conflicts with wide-scale repercussions, like the breakaway of England under Henry VIII, the revolt of the Seventeen Provinces in the Habsburg Netherlands and the establishment of the Dutch Republic, and the Thirty Years' War. But the violence of the conflict during this period is also a reflection of the fervency of people's religious convictions. We tend to imagine the early modern period as a time when science as we know it was born, when a recognizably modern view of the world emerged, but it was also a time of strong—and conflicting—spiritual beliefs. It requires some effort for the modern secular mind to grasp the extent to which, in early modern religious thought, worldly events were imbued with spiritual significance.

The conviction that the physical world has spiritual significance did not, of course, originate with early modern Christian thinkers. It has a long pedigree going back to Saint Augustine and well beyond. In book 1, chapter 4 of *De Doctrina Christiana*, for example, Saint Augustine wrote:

Suppose, then, we were travelers in a foreign land, who could not live in contentment except in our own native country, and if, unhappy because of that traveling abroad and desirous of ending our wretchedness, we planned to return home, it would be necessary to use some means of transportation, either by land or sea, to enable us to reach the land we were to enjoy. But if the pleasantness of the journey and the very movement of the vehicles were to delight us and turn us aside to enjoy the things which we ought, instead, merely to use, and were to confuse us by false pleasure, we would be unwilling to end our journey quickly and would be alienated from the land whose pleasantness would make us truly happy. Just so, wanderers from God on the road of this mortal life, if we wish to return to our native country where we can be happy, we must use this world, and not enjoy it, so that the "invisible attributes" of God may be clearly seen, "being understood through the things that are made," that is, that through what is corporeal and temporal we may comprehend the eternal and spiritual.[1]

This traditional sense that the true significance of the physical world is spiritual played a central role in much early modern religious thought. Protestantism put an individual "spin" on the notion, though. One of the fundamentals that distinguished Protestants from Catholics was that Protestants believed in a *personal* relationship with God. Catholics could rely on the church and the clergy as mediators between them and God. For Puritans, Calvinists, and Lutherans, God was an integral part of the daily events of their personal lives. Look at this passage from Martin Luther's *Der Kleine Katechismus* (*The Small Catechism*), intended as an instructional book for children, first printed in 1529:

I believe that God has made me and all creatures; that He has given me my body and soul, eyes, ears, and all my members, my reason and all my senses, and still takes care of them. He also gives me clothing and shoes, food and drink, house and home, wife and children, land, animals, and all I have. He richly and daily provides me with all that I need to support this body and life. He defends me against all danger and guards and protects me from all evil.[2]

Notice the central tenet here: daily events are the result of direct intervention by God, not of random physical causes. In other words, not only is the world itself, and all the events in it, imbued with a spiritual significance, but that significance manifests itself in the events of individual lives. All this is very different from the viewpoint that was emerging in natural philosophy—or, as we would now call it, science.

1. St. Augustine, *Christian Instruction*, trans. John J. Gavigan, OSA, The Fathers of the Church: A New Translation (Patristic Series) 2 (2002, rpt.; Washington, D.C.: The Catholic University of America Press, 1950), 1, 29–30.
2. *Luther's Small Catechism, with Explanation, Standard English Version* (St. Louis, Mo.: Concordia Publishing House, 2008), 15–16.

## Science

The period during which science in Europe had its beginnings lasted almost a century and a half and can be bracketed by two famous publications:

The *De revolutionibus orbium coelestium libri VI* (*Six Books Concerning the Revolutions of the Heavenly Orbs*), published by Nicolaus Copernicus in 1543 (21 years before Reverend Ólafur's birth); and

The *Philosophiae Naturalis Principia Mathematica* (*Mathematical Principles of Natural Philosophy*) published by Isaac Newton in 1687 (48 years after Reverend Ólafur's death).

Science is more than just technology. It is an epistemology, a way of perceiving the world—a world view. Look at the following from Leonardo da Vinci's *Notebooks*:

Do they not know that my subjects require for their exposition experience rather than the words of others? ... Experience is never at fault; it is only your judgment that is in error in promising itself such results from experience as are not caused by our experiments. For having given a beginning, what follows from it must necessarily be a natural development of such a beginning, unless it has been subject to a contrary influence.... There is no certainty where one can neither apply any of the mathematical sciences nor any of those which are based upon the mathematical sciences.[3]

Leonardo was writing a couple of generations before Reverend Ólafur (Leonardo died in 1519, 45 years before Reverend Ólafur was born), but the convictions he expressed regarding how one achieves certain knowledge about the world had "gone viral" (so to speak) and were strongly held by many in Reverend Ólafur's time.

3. Edward Maccurdy, trans. *The Notebooks of Leonardo Da Vinci* (New York: George Braziller, 1955), 58, 64, 611.

The emergence of science, with its beginnings in natural philosophy, can be seen as a gradual process by which the physical world was emptied of spiritual significance and became purely and simply material—became the "natural" world as we now think of it today. From this "natural" perspective, events in the world, and in people's individual lives, were not the result of God's direct intervention but of natural forces. John Calvin could write (in his *Psychopannychia*), "Let us therefore conclude, with Solomon, that all these things are beyond the reach of human reason. But if we would have any certainty, let us run to the law and the testimony [of the Bible], where are the truth and the ways of the Lord." For Leonardo, however, and for natural philosophers like him, certainty of knowledge came about not through the Bible, not through the word or God, but through human reason and the mechanical and mathematical sciences.[4]

It is in this sense that the two major forces of the early modern period in Europe—the religious and the scientific—were pulling against each other. On the one hand, the powerful religious faith of the period led people to feel that God was immanent in both the world at large and in their personal lives, and that world events were the result of God's direct intervention. On the other hand, the convictions of nascent science (of natural philosophy) led people to believe that the world was a material place in which events were the result of impersonal natural forces that could be measured and controlled.

These two diametrically opposed convictions fit together in ways that sometimes seem contradictory to the modern mind,

4. *Selected Works of John Calvin Tracts and Letters Vol. 3, Tracts Part 3*, ed. Henry Beveridge and Jules Bonnet, trans. Henry Beveridge, David Constable, and M.R. Gilchrist, 1849 (Grand Rapids, Mich.: Baker, 1983), 424.

but in order to better understand the early modern period in general, and Reverend Ólafur and *The Travels* in particular, it is important to be aware of how these two ways of looking at—and experiencing—the world could be combined. This sometimes odd combinational process can be seen in two of the most famous natural philosophers of early modern Europe: Johannes Kepler and Isaac Newton.

### Johannes Kepler

Johannes Kepler (1571–1630, born 7 years after Reverend Ólafur, died 9 years before Reverend Ólafur) is best known today for his discovery that the planets move around the sun in elliptical rather than circular orbits, and for the three laws of planetary motion that he developed. Before this, the heavens were seen as being profoundly different from the earth: the heavens were considered a spiritual realm, and, as such, perfect, so it followed naturally that the planets should move in circular orbits—as the circle was considered a perfect form. The traditional Ptolemaic system of cycles and epicycles described these perfect orbits. Kepler's discovery that the planets did not move in circular orbits represents a profoundly radical shift, for if the planets did not move in perfectly circular orbits, then they were, by definition, not perfect, and it must follow that the heavens themselves were imperfect. If the heavens were flawed, they could not be the realm of divine spiritual perfection they were thought to be. The heavens thus were no longer a sacrosanct realm but rather a merely physical one, in which natural laws prevailed. This was profoundly revolutionary.

Given all this, Kepler is often portrayed as an early scientist, a man ahead of his time, striving mightily to discover the underlying scientific laws of the physical universe. Things were not that simple, however.

Kepler began his career as a theologian. He was a profoundly religious man, and, like many men of his time, he believed the world was like a great book in which the "words" of God could be read. He believed, for example, that the Holy Trinity could be read in the physical qualities of a sphere: God the Father in the center of the sphere; Christ the Son in the circumference of the sphere; the Holy Ghost in the intervening space between. Kepler never used the word "laws" to describe the regularities he discovered in the planets' orbits. He perceived the regularities described by his three laws as examples of grand celestial harmonies, of the hidden words of God revealed.

Believing in the hidden spiritual regularities of the world as he did, Kepler was as much an astrologer as he was an astronomer. His first publication (in 1601) was *De Fundamentis Astrologiae Certioribus* (*Concerning the More Certain Fundamentals of Astrology*). In 1627 (the year Reverend Ólafur was abducted by Barbary corsairs), Kepler published the *Tabulae Rudolphinae* (*The Rudolphine Tables*), a collection of star charts. Based on the observations of the Danish astronomer Tycho Brahe (with whom Kepler had worked), the *Tabulae* contained the most accurate star charts produced up until that time. The *Tabulae* were invaluable as an aid to navigation, but they were also used in attempts to cast more precise horoscopes. Towards the end of his life, Kepler worked for one of the Holy Roman emperor's generals, Albrecht von Wallenstein. Among other things, von Wallenstein undertook to supply Kepler with a printing press, but in return von Wallenstein expected Kepler to provide him with detailed and accurate horoscopes.

Kepler, then, was not simply a proto-scientist, not simply a man ahead of his time. He spent much of his life closely observing the natural world and working out the details of what we now think of as natural laws, yet at the same time he perceived the presence of God, of the spiritual, in all things. This same sort of complicated and seemingly contradictory mix can also be seen in Isaac Newton.

## Isaac Newton

Isaac Newton (1643–1727, born 4 years after Reverend Ólafur's death) is, of course, considered one of the great fathers of science. This is undeniably true in a direct sense: his three laws of motion, his theory of gravity, his invention of calculus, and much else are all matters of record. The popular image of Newton as a brilliant, modern-minded scientist, however, is an oversimplification.

In 1936, John Maynard Keynes, the English economist, bought at auction a collection of Newton's papers considered to be "of no scientific value." These papers revealed that Newton was preoccupied with the Bible, with what today would be considered some of the more mystical aspects of Christianity, and with alchemy. In fact, Newton wrote more about religious matters than he did about science. After reading the Newton papers he had bought, Keynes concluded, "Newton was not the first of the age of reason: he was the last of the magicians."

Newton wrote voluminously about the Bible, producing textual criticism and, among other things, setting dates for Christ's crucifixion (AD 33) and the end of the world (no earlier than 2060). He also pursued alchemy in the classic search for the philosopher's stone and the elixir of life, quite possible poisoning himself in the process (analysis of some of Newton's hair revealed that it contained high trace amounts of mercury, perhaps explaining his well-known mental quirks).

Among other things, Newton showed that the same set of "laws" that governed the motions of the planets also governed the motions of objects on Earth, and so demonstrated in a rigorous mathematical fashion that the way the "heavens" worked was identical to the way the earth worked. But his perspective on this was not modern. He is famously quoted as saying, "Gravity explains the motions of the planets, but it cannot explain who set the planets in motion. God governs all things and knows all that is or can be done." Like Kepler, Newton worked to elucidate the underlying natural laws of the universe, but, at the same time, he also believed that God was immanent in events, and that He created, ordered, and ruled the natural world.

In *Observations Concerning the Inflexions of the Rays of Light, and the Colours Made Thereby*, in part 1 of *Opticks* (published in 1704), he wrote:

The main Business of natural Philosophy is to argue from Phænomena without feigning Hypotheses, and to deduce Causes from Effects, till we come to the very first Cause, which certainly is not mechanical.... Whence is it that Nature doth nothing in vain; and whence arises all that Order and Beauty which we see in the World? To what end are Comets, and whence is it that Planets move all one and the same way in Orbs concentrick, while Comets move all manner of ways in Orbs very excentrick; and what hinders the fix'd Stars from falling upon one another? How came the Bodies of Animals to be contrived with so much Art, and for what ends were their several Parts? Was the Eye contrived without Skill in Opticks, and the Ear without Knowledge of Sounds? ... And these things being rightly dispatch'd, does it not appear from Phænomena that there is a Being incorporeal, living, intelligent, omnipresent, who in infinite Space, as it were in his Sensory, sees the things themselves intimately, and throughly perceives them, and comprehends them wholly by their immediate presence to himself.... And though every true Step made in this Philosophy brings us not immediately to the Knowledge of the first Cause, yet it brings us nearer to it, and on that account is to be highly valued.[5]

5. Isaac Newton, *Opticks: or, a Treatise of the Reflections, Refractions, Inflections and Colours of Light*, Fourth Edition, corrected (London: printed for William Innys at the west-end of St. Paul's, MDCCXXX [1730]), 370.

The combination that one can see in Kepler and Newton (born 72 years apart)—on the one hand, a preoccupation with accurately measuring and describing natural phenomena, and on the other hand, seeing the direct presence of God in everything—can strike modern readers as odd, but it was typical of the early modern period. One can also see this sort of mix in the literature of the time.

### Literature

Early Modern literature is a complex topic in its own right. It was a combination of various elements, fed by, among other things, the Renaissance humanists' abiding interest in classical antiquity, the religious preoccupations of the Reformation/Counter-Reformation, and the discoveries that resulted from exploration of both the "New" and the "Old" Worlds. Drama reached new heights in England, Spain, and Portugal. Poetry and reflective essays flourished. The Bible was translated into various European languages. Cervantes created what many consider to be the first successful novel.

One result of the exploration of the "New" and "Old" worlds was a growth in travel literature. Early travel literature often contained magic and marvels (like the mermaids Columbus's crew were reported to have seen). Over time, however, travel literature became an important source of knowledge in natural philosophy. Francis Bacon himself promoted it as a basis for compiling "natural" knowledge. By the end of seventeenth century, travel literature was considered a legitimate resource (there were, for example, extensive travel reports in the British Royal Society's *Philosophical Transactions*).

One example can stand as the type for this sort of writing. In 1688, an English translation of a travel book by the Frenchman Guy Tachard was published in London, with the lengthy title *A relation of the voyage to Siam: performed by six Jesuits, sent*

by the French King, to the Indies and China, in the year, 1685: with
their astrological observations, and their remarks of natural philosophy, geography, hydrography, and history: published in the original, by the express orders of His Most Christian Majesty: and now
made English, and illustrated with sculptures. This work recounts
a voyage made by Jesuit priests, yet the title specifies that these
priests reported on "natural philosophy, geography, hydrography, and history"—on what we would now consider the natural
world—rather than on religious or spiritual issues.

At the same time as this "naturalizing" approach was being
adopted, however, there was also a strain of more spiritual literature that could perhaps be loosely termed as belonging to an
*imitatio Christi* tradition. In the early fifteenth century, a book
titled *De imitatione Christi* appeared (likely written by Thomas
à Kempis). Among other things, it encouraged the reader to
focus on the spiritual aspect of life rather than the material.
This focus on things spiritual—fed from various traditions—is
threaded through much early modern literature, culminating
(in English, at least) in works like Bunyan's *The Pilgrim's Progress from This World to That Which Is to Come* (published in
1678, 39 years after Reverend Ólafur's death), a work following
the venerable traditions of allegory, in which the physical journey of Christian (the Everyman protagonist) from the City of
Destruction to the Celestial City stands for the progress of the
soul from baptism through earthly trials to heaven.

In 1626 (the year before Reverend Ólafur was abducted),
Francis Bacon's *The New Atlantis* was published, a work of uto-
pian fiction that described an imaginary society built upon the
principles of natural philosophy that Bacon expounded in the
*Novum Organum*. The beginning of *The New Atlantis* provides
an instructive example of how the two traditions—naturalistic
and spiritual—get intertwined. Here is how the book begins:

We sailed from Peru, where we had continued by the space of one whole year, for China and Japan, by the South Sea, taking with us victuals for twelve months; and had good winds from the east, though soft and weak, for five months' space and more. But then the wind came about, and settled in the west for many days, so as we could make little or no way, and were sometimes in purpose to turn back. But then again there arose strong and great winds from the south, with a point east; which carried us up, for all that we could do, toward the north: by which time our victuals failed us, though we had made good spare of them. So that finding ourselves, in the midst of the greatest wilderness of waters in the world, without victual, we gave ourselves up for lost men, and prepared for death. Yet we did lift up our hearts and voices to God above, who showeth His wonders in the deep; beseeching Him of His mercy that as in the beginning He discovered the face of the deep, and brought forth dry land, so He would now discover land to us, that we might not perish.

And it came to pass that the next day about evening we saw within a kenning before us, toward the north, as if it were thick clouds, which did put us in some hope of land, knowing how that part of the South Sea was utterly unknown, and might have islands or continents that hitherto were not come to light.[6]

This extract illustrates the seemingly contradictory combination of the naturalistic and the spiritual. Notice the careful attention paid to detail about, and measurement of, the natural world at the beginning (emphasis added): "We sailed from Peru, where we had continued by the space of *one whole year*, for China and Japan, by the South Sea, taking with us *victuals for twelve months*; and had *good winds from the east*, though soft and weak, *for five month's space* and more. But then the wind came about, and *settled in the west for many days*.... But then again there arose strong and great winds from the south, *with a point east*."

6. Gerard B. Wegemer, ed., *The New Atlantis (1626) by Francis Bacon* (Irving, Tex.: University of Dallas, Center for Thomas More Studies, 2003), 1.

Except for the slightly archaic English, the narrative so far sounds almost entirely modern—and entirely naturalistic. This is followed, however, by: "We did lift up our hearts and voices to God above, who showeth His wonders in the deep; beseeching Him ... so He would now discover land to us.... And it came to pass that the next day about evening we saw within a kenning before us, toward the north, as it were thick clouds, which did put us in some hope of land." In other words, God intervened directly in events.

The early modern period, then, was a transitional period in which the traditional Christian spiritual perspective was giving way to a more naturalistic one, and so these two perspectives existed side by side in a complex balance. At such a period, the seemingly contradictory combination of the spiritual and the naturalistic, foreign though it might be to the modern secular mind, was, perhaps, inevitable. It was certainly typical of much early modern writing. *The Travels* is no exception. Reverend Ólafur is a keen-eyed observer, and he relates naturalistic details carefully and accurately. At the same time, though, he focuses with equal force on the spiritual import of events.

The following excerpt from Reverend Ólafur's narrative (chapter XXII, in which Holland is described) illustrates the scrupulous attention Reverend Ólafur paid to naturalistic detail:

Ships lay at anchor [on canals] amongst the houses and not outside except when cargo is loaded or unloaded. Where the Dutch first see a sandy spit or shallow shoal, they shovel out a big outlet and throw the clay from the sea bottom up on both sides. After a year, the clay is hard as stone. The towns which I visited were built on such ridges of clay. Across the canals that are thus formed in these towns are surprisingly huge bridges made with great skill. Some of these can be drawn up and down in order to let ships pass. On both sorts, horses are ridden and carriages driven. To maintain these canals, ten men from the town are normally retained, who go along these canals in shallow boats with poles in their hands. They wear boots which come up under their armpits. At the lower end of their poles they have what look like wool-cards with five or six wide teeth made of iron. They dredge the canals and place the mud or clay that comes out wherever the town's authorities tell them. After a year, it is hard as stone, and then new houses are built. And so the towns expand year after year, with the dates being marked on each house door.

An excerpt from one of the letters that accompany Reverend Ólafur's narrative serves as another illustration of the same careful, detailed naturalistic description. Here is Guttormur Hallsson's portrayal of his life as a slave in Algiers:

The hardest time in this country, when the labour is most difficult, is from the winter moon in November (the first month of winter) until the seventh week has passed of summer. During the rest of the year, when I am not ploughing, I must walk the town selling water, which is a difficult labour and one that many Christian people must endure. We must pay our masters a certain amount of money every day. If we can get more than that amount, it is to our profit, and we can use it to feed and clothe ourselves. But if we cannot earn the required amount, then it is taken out of our clothing and our food.

This careful attention to naturalistic detail is counter-weighted by an equal concern for spiritual matters. The following excerpts from Reverend Ólafur's narrative and from one of the letters (Jón Jónsson's, in which he describes events that happened in Algiers) illustrate this spiritual aspect:

Chapter I (which contains only the following): In this chapter Reverend Ólafur Egilsson describes how, in the Old Testament, warnings appeared before punishment came.

Chapter II (which contains only the following): Reverend Ólafur Egilsson explains signs and events which happened here in Iceland, mainly in the Westman Islands, which were warnings for what happened later, but of which nobody took notice.

**Chapter IX (in which a storm at sea during the voyage from Iceland to North Africa is described):** The evil pirates took the decision to slaughter a ram (a very fat one) as a sacrifice either to the Devil or to some one of their idols—I do not know which. They cut the ram into two pieces and threw a piece over each side of the ship, and the storm became calm within a few hours.

**Jón Jónsson's letter (in which events that happened in Algiers are described):** The wizard had meanwhile been preparing himself with his secret magical skill. He walked to the port and threw into the sea a small drum with magical characters inscribed on it. Then the sea started to toss and was suddenly gripped by a powerful storm with waves so strong that one Spanish ship was driven against another, and they were broken all to pieces.

Notice how the world depicted in these excerpts is full of magic and divine (or malign) intervention. It is not at all the naturalistic world we moderns take for granted. Such a world is common in early modern writing, though. Recall chapter II: "signs and events which happened here in Iceland, mainly in the Westman Islands, which were warnings for what happened later, but of which nobody took notice." To get a sense of what, exactly, these "signs and events" might have been, one needs only to look at Shakespeare's *Macbeth* (Act 2, Scene 3):

MacDuff and Lennox enter at Macbeth's castle gate just after the murder of King Duncan.

> **Lennox:** The night has been unruly: where we lay,
> Our chimneys were blown down; and, as they say,
> Lamentings were heard i'th'air, strange screams of death,
> And prophesying with accents terrible
> Of dire combustion, and confus'd events,
> New hatch'd to th' woeful time, the obscure bird

Clamour'd the livelong night: some say, the earth
Was feverous, and did shake.[7]

These are not simple, natural events; they are imbued with spir-itual portent.

The spiritual aspect of *The Travels*, however, consists of more than just these sorts of observations of magical events. Look at the following excerpts from both Guttormur Hallsson's and Jón Jónsson's letters.

**From Guttormur Hallsson's letter:** Preachers, parents, relatives, friends, brothers, sisters, and all our true Christian fellows from oth-er parts of Iceland, please pray for us to the living God in your daily prayers, that God may have pity on us and rescue us from this yoke of slavery that the ungodly and wicked tyrants have placed upon us, if it is not asked against His merciful will. We are like the prodigal son who squandered his inheritance and did not return to his father's house until hunger and need drove him to it. Oh, Father, look upon us mercifully. Help us, God, and bring us salvation, because of your glory and great name, and forgive us our sins. Amen.

**From Jón Jónsson's letter:** We ask you now to forgive, in the name of God, our childhood disobediences, our unruliness and our faults, for we would wish to be included in your warm prayers and interces-sions unto God, trusting that our deserved exile and proscription will end well, since the parents' blessing builds the children a house. We see here daily indications of God's mercy, and perhaps your prayers too, for we have kept our Christian faith, and we are together in one city, not far off from each other, and see each other almost daily. In this, God's mercy has rewarded us, for which He should have eternal thanks.

Notice the underlying premise of these extracts. Events in the world are not random, not due to impersonal natural forces;

7. Kenneth Muir, ed., *Macbeth* by William Shakespeare (N.Y.: Methuen, 1984), 61–62.

they are the result of God's will. Consequently, the captivity of the letter writers must also be due to God's will, and so rescue lies in God's hands—accessible through supplicating prayer.

In *The Travels*, Reverend Ólafur and the other Icelandic captives must grapple with one of the most profound and disturbing of spiritual issues. In Book I of *Paradise Lost* (published in 1667, 28 years after Reverend Ólafur's death), John Milton wrote:

> … What in me is dark
> Illumine, what is low raise and support;
> That to the highth of this great Argument
> I may assert th' Eternal Providence,
> And justifie the wayes of God to men.[8]

In his own way, Reverend Ólafur, too, tried to "justifie the wayes of God" to himself and his fellow Icelanders, who were trying to cope with the trauma of the corsair raid. The dilemma that Reverend Ólafur and the others faced was this: if God can, and does, intervene in events, then why are good, faithful people subject to terrible misfortune? In grappling with this issue, Reverend Ólafur relies on the Book of Job. In *The Travels* he refers to Job multiple times—because the Book of Job deals with "pointless" suffering.

In Job 42:2, Job says to God: "I know that thou canst do every thing and that no thought can be withholden from thee." In Job 8:20, Bildad the Shuhite says: "Behold, God will not cast away a perfect man, neither will he help the evil doers." The problem is that, in the Book of Job, God apparently does "cast away a perfect man" and "help the evil doers" when he allows

---

8. Barbara K. Lewalski, ed., *John Milton: Paradise Lost* (Malden, Mass.: Blackwell, 2007), book I, the Argument, 12.

Job's possessions to be destroyed and his offspring to be killed, despite the fact that Job is a righteous man.

Job's response to his misfortune is not to rail against God, but to say: "Naked came I out of my mother's womb, and naked shall I return thither: the Lord gave and the Lord hath taken away" (Job 1:21). And when his wife urges him to "curse God and die," Job responds: "Shall we receive good at the hand of God, and shall we not receive evil?" (Job 2:10).

When Reverend Ólafur wrote *The Travels*, he had returned home to Iceland, but his wife and children were still in North Africa, along with the other Icelandic captives, and he had no way of knowing if he would ever see any of them again. The way in which he attempts to come to terms with his personal tragedy is similar to Job's. Here is how he concludes *The Travels*:

> My dear, beloved reader and good friend, I must confess that, because of the loss of my wife and children, whom God himself heals, I cannot talk or write as I want or should....
>
> But the will of God decides everything. My choice in these matters, in these mournful days of distress, is none else than to flee to the Lord and to still hope for His mercy, both for me and my family, and all others who have walked or will walk the path of distress and adversity. The Holy Spirit may be called the Eternal Father, for I believe that He will not remove His fatherly heart from His children although He still punishes them.

When Reverend Ólafur writes, "But the will of God decides everything. My choice in these matters, in these mournful days of distress, is none else than to flee to the Lord and to still hope for His mercy," he is writing in the same vein as Isaac Newton ("God governs all things and knows all that is or can be done"); and Martin Luther ("[God] gives me clothing and shoes, food and drink, house and home, wife and children, land, animals, and all I have"). Since God directly manages the events of the world, He is the source of both fortune and misfortune, and so He is not only the cause of misfortune but also its remedy.

To the modern secular reader, the biblical references that conclude most chapters of Reverend Ólafur's narrative may seem artificial, following his careful, practical observations as they do, as if they were just tacked on at the end for form's sake. They were not. Reverend Ólafur's observations of the world he traveled through may have been practical and prosaic—he clearly was, in many ways, a practical and prosaic man—but the significance of what he experienced remained for him spiritual, and the way he made sense of events was through his understanding of God's will in the world. For him, no doubt, the mixing of the practical and the spiritual that can strike modern secular readers as anomalous did not feel out of balance in the least, nor would it have for his contemporary readers.

*The Travels of Reverend Ólafur Egilsson*, then, presents the modern secular reader with a combination that may at first seem somewhat confusing—the unlikely mix of careful naturalistic observation and descriptions of events alongside deeply spiritual interpretations of events—but by now it should be clear how typical this mix is of much early modern writing. If the reader keeps the historical context in mind, *The Travels* can open up a window into the past, allowing a view of both outer and inner life in the seventeenth century. It provides us with an exceptional opportunity to understand the day-to-day workings of seventeenth century civilization, both in the Maghreb and in Europe, while also granting us a firsthand glimpse into the seventeenth century European mind and so allowing us to better understand how people of that period thought and felt about events. And that, surely, is a remarkable and instructive combination.

# Suggestions for Further Reading

THIS LIST is not meant to be exhaustive. It is merely a collection of suggested readings (with annotations) for those who may wish to explore further the background to the Tyrkjaránið. All these books are either very readable or very informative, or both.

Auchterlonie, Paul. *Encountering Islam. Joseph Pitts: An English Slave in 17th-Century Algiers and Mecca.* London: Arabian Publishing, 2012. Contains the full text of Joseph Pitts's captivity narrative (*A True and Faithful Account of the Religion and Manners of the Mohammetans ... with an Account of the Author's Being Taken Captive*) originally published in 1704. Pitts, who "turned Turk," was the first Englishman to visit Mecca and write about it. This is a "critical edition" and so contains extensive explanatory footnotes and a very useful, detailed introduction.

Clissold, Stephen. *The Barbary Slaves.* New York: Barnes and Noble Books, 1992. An overview of the Barbary states, with a focus on slavery. Includes sections on life in the bagnios, escapes, renegados, and ransoms.

Dan, Pierre. *Histoire de Barbarie, et de ses Corsaires Des royaumes et des villes d'Alger de Tunis de Salé de Tripoly. Divisée en six livres ou il est traitté de leur gouvernement de leurs moeurs de leurs cruautez de leurs brigandages* [*History of the Barbary and of its Corsairs and Kingdoms and of the cities of Algiers, Tunis, Salé, and Tripoli. Divided into six books wherein is treated their government, their mores, their cruelties, and their robberies*]. New Delhi: Isha Books, 2013.

(For simplicity's sake, we have modernized the spelling of this title for English readers, replacing the Latinate letter *v* that appears in the original in some of the words with the more familiar *u*—"Tvnis," for example, is rendered as "Tunis.") A facsimile reproduction of the second edition (1649) of Father Dan's monumental work on the Barbary states produced at a reasonable cost by an Indian publisher. If you can handle the old French (especially the orthography), this book is well worth investing in for its incredible wealth of detail.

Davies, John. *The history of Algiers and its slavery with many remarkable particularities of Africk, written by the Sieur Emanuel d' Aranda, sometime a slave there, English'd by John Davies* (published in 1666). Ann Arbor, Mich.: University of Michigan, Digital Library Production Service. http://quod.lib.umich.edu/e/eebo/ A25743.0001.001?view=toc. A seventeenth century English translation of Emanuel d'Aranda's *Relation de la captivité du sieur Emanuel d' Aranda mené esclave à Alger en l'an 1640 et mise en liberté l'an 1642* [*Story of the Captivity of Emanuel d' Aranda, Enslaved in Algiers in 1640 and liberated in 1642*] available online as a free download through the University of Michigan's Early English Books Text Creation Partnership. Contains a wealth of fascinating detail about what it was like to be a slave in Algiers during the seventeenth century.

Davies, Robert C. *Christian Slaves, Muslim Masters: White Slavery in the Mediterranean, the Barbary Coast and Italy, 1500–1800.* Houndmills, U.K.: Palgrave Macmillan, 2004. A wide-ranging, serious study of corsairs and slavery, including interesting sections on total numbers of Europeans enslaved in Barbary states, what the experience of being a slave was like, and how European powers, too, used corsairing and slavery as instruments of state policy.

Ekin, Des. *The Stolen Village: Baltimore and the Barbary Pirates.* Dublin: O'Brien Press, 2008. A fascinating and very readable account of the attack by Barbary corsairs on Baltimore, Ireland, in 1631. The book provides a gripping account of the raid itself and of the experiences of the captives enslaved in Algiers.

Fuchs, Barbara, and Aaron J. Ilika. "*The Great Bagnios of Algiers*" and "*The Great Sultana*": *Two Plays of Captivity.* Philadelphia,

Penn.: University of Pennsylvania Press, 2010. Contains modern English translations of two plays by Miguel de Cervantes, both dealing with slavery. The events of *The Great Bagnios of Algiers* take place in Algiers; those of *The Great Sultana* in Constantinople. The story of the former contains many of the same details related in the captive's tale in chapters 39–41 of *Don Quixote*.

Garcés, Maria Antonia. *Cervantes in Algiers: A Captive's Tale*. Nashville, Tenn.: Vanderbilt University Press, 2005. A thorough and very informative account of the experiences of Miguel de Cervantes (author of *Don Quixote*) as a slave in Algiers for five years (1575–80).

Garcés, Maria Antonia, and Diana De Armas. *An Early Modern Dialogue with Islam: Antonio de Sosa's Topography of Algiers (1612)*. Notre Dame, Ind.: University of Notre Dame Press, 2011. A translation of the first book of Antonio de Sosa's *Topographia, e historia general de Argel* [*Topography and General History of Algiers*], including an extensive discussion of the historical background to the book. The original sixteenth century Spanish is rendered into lucid English.

Greengrass, Mark. *Christendom Destroyed: Europe 1517–1648*. New York: Viking, 2014. A lengthy, highly detailed discussion of just about every imaginable aspect of the period.

Jamieson, Alan G. *Lords of the Sea: A History of the Barbary Corsairs*. London: Reaktion Books, 2012. A general account of the Barbary corsairs. Very readable.

Karlson, Gunnar. *Iceland's 1,100 Years: History of a Marginal Society*. London: Hurst and Company, 2000. An overview of Icelandic history from its founding by Norse settlers in the ninth century until the present. Very informative.

Lewis, Bernard. *Islam in History: Ideas, People, and Events in the Middle East*. Chicago: Open Court Publishing Company, 1993. Contains an interesting chapter on the Tyrkjaránið. Lewis is a prominent scholar of Islam.

Matar, Nabil. *Europe through Arab Eyes, 1578–1727*. New York: Columbia University Press, 2008. A collection of translated travel writings from the Muslim world, providing some fascinating glimpses of Europe from "the other side."

Spencer, William. *Algiers in the Age of the Corsairs*. Norman, Okla.: University of Oklahoma Press, 1976. A detailed and very informative discussion of Algiers during the period.

Teyssier, Paul. *Esclave à Alger: récit de captivité de João Mascarenhas (1621–1626)* [*A Slave in Algiers: the Captivity Narrative of João Mascarenhas (1621–1626)*]. Paris: Éditions Chandeigne, 1993. A translation of Mascarenhas' captivity narrative *Memorável Relação da Perda da Nau Conceição* [*A Memorable Account of the Loss of the Ship Conceição*]. The original seventeenth century Portuguese is translated into wonderfully clear French.

Tinniswood, Adrian. *Pirates of Barbary: Corsairs, Conquests and Captivity in the Seventeenth-Century Mediterranean*. New York: Riverhead Books, 2011. A wide-ranging, informative, very readable discussion of the Barbary corsairs and the system that supported them.

Thomson, Janice E. *Mercenaries, Pirates, and Sovereigns*. Princeton: Princeton University Press, 1996. A fascinating general exploration of the evolution of state-controlled violence, including (in passing) the role of corsairs and the Barbary states.

Vitkus, Daniel J. *Piracy, Slavery, and Redemption: Barbary Captivity Narratives from Early Modern England*. New York: Columbia University Press, 2001. A collection of seven English captivity narratives of varying types and lengths, ranging in dates from 1589 to 1704. Together, they provide a revealing mosaic of the times. Contains an informative introduction by Nabil Matar.

Wilson, Peter Lamborn. *Pirate Utopias: Moorish Corsairs and European Renegadoes*. New York: Autonomedia, 2003. A general discussion of Barbary corsairs. Very readable.

# Index

233

*The Travels of Reverend Ólafur Egilsson: The Story of the Barbary Corsair Raid on Iceland in 1627* was designed in Adobe Jensen Pro with Carter Sans display type and composed by Kachergis Book Design of Pittsboro, North Carolina. It was printed on 60-pound Natural Eggshell and bound by McNaughton & Gunn of Saline, Michigan.